DIVING
BELIZE

DIVING
BELIZE
BY NED MIDDLETON

AQUA QUEST PUBLICATIONS, INC. ■ NEW YORK

PUBLISHER'S NOTE

The Aqua Quest *Diving* series offers extensive information on dive sites as well as topside activities.

At the time of publication, the information contained in this book was determined to be as accurate and up-to-date as possible. The reader should bear in mind, however, that dive site terrain and landmarks change due to weather or construction. In addition, new dive shops, restaurants, hotels and stores can open and existing ones close. Telephone numbers are subject to change as are government regulations.

The publisher welcomes the reader's comments and assistance to help ensure the accuracy of future editions of this book.

Good diving and enjoy your stay!

Library of Congress Cataloging-in-Publication Data

Middleton, Ned, 1950-
    Diving Belize / by Ned Middleton.
        p.   cm.   — (Aqua Quest diving series)
    Includes index.
    ISBN 1-881652-01-7 : $18.95
    1. Scuba diving—Belize—Guidebooks. 2. Marine biology—Belize. 3. Belize—Guidebooks.
    I. Title. II. Series.
GV840.S48M52   1994
797.2'3—dc20

Cover: The wreck of the *Ermlund* sits on top of the reef a few hundred yards (meters) north of Half Moon Caye on Lighthouse Reef. While most of Belize's shipwrecks are not diveable, they are dramatic and add to the atmosphere of the offshore atoll reefs. Photo: Ned Middleton.

Title page: The Great Blue Hole, one of the most astounding dive sites in the world is located right in the center of of Lighthouse Reef. Photo: Ned Middleton.

This edition revised in January, 1998.
Printed in Hong Kong
10 9 8 7 6 5 4 3 2

Design by Richard Liu.

ACKNOWLEDGEMENTS

This book is dedicated to the memory of

JAMIE CHOULES
(1950-1987)

and divers like him

*"The world is a richer place
for his having passed through."*

The writing of this book would not have been possible without the assistance and patience of a great number of people. If you visit Belize, you will certainly meet some of them. If you are fortunate, you will meet all of them. Of course, any errors or omissions in this volume are strictly mine.

I would like to single out Jacques-Yves Cousteau for his assistance in setting the record straight with some delicate points covered in Chapter VIII. To Captain Cousteau and all those whose names appear below, my sincere thanks.

Andy Barrett, Reef Divers Ltd., San Pedro; Heather Bolei, divemaster, Lighthouse Reef Resort; Ray Bowers, owner and captain of the *Reef Roamer II;* John Brown, JBI Asset Management Ltd.; Vic Butcher, former chief diver, St. George's Caye; Linda Carter, scuba instructor, San Pedro; Sam Drennan MBE, DFC, AFC-Army Air Corps; Jayne Dunlop, librarian, Royal Geographical Society; Michael Fairweather, former captain of the *Reef Roamer II*; Bill Fisher, Manta Resort, Glover's Reef; Allan Forman, Coral Beach Hotel, San Pedro; Linda Galipeau, Manta Resort, Glover's Reef; Janet Gibson, Belize Audubon Society; Steve Greenway, underwater photographer; Shaun Houck, owner and captain of the *Dulcé II*; Sid Kyte, Royal Air Force; Kendall McDonald, journalist and diver; Beverley Mercier, Island Property Management, San Pedro; Joe Miller, Island Photos, San Pedro; Dick Parham, Isla Bonita Hotel, San Pedro; Larry and Kris Parker, Reef Divers Ltd./Island Explorers Ltd., San Pedro; Hugh Parkey, formerly of the Turneffe Island Lodge; Peter Raines, London School of Pharmacy; Louise Rossignol, Fondation Cousteau, Paris; Don Seruntine, Tackle Box Bar, San Pedro; Ned Simpson, Lighthouse Reef Resort; Cal Syme, captain of the *Manta IV*; Steve Thayer, The Parachute Regiment, Freddie Waight, Ambergris Caye; Richie Woods, marine biologist, Ambergris Caye; Charlie Worthington, San Pedro Grill Restaurant.

Contents

CHAPTER VIII

LIGHTHOUSE REEF 76

CHAPTER IX

BANCO CHINCHORRO: *Mexico* 96

CHAPTER X

MARINE LIFE 110

FOREWORD

My first visit to Belize was in 1987 when I was stationed there for six months. I was already well aware of the country's reputation as a first-class diving destination and took every opportunity to discover the unspoiled beauty of Belize's reefs for myself. Although I have dived worldwide, Belize went straight to my heart. The diving is superb, the food excellent and varied, the accommodations diverse enough to suit every pocket, and the tropical climate is great. On top of all this, the people are just fabulous and everyone is keen to make the visitor most welcome. I have returned to Belize every year since that first trip.

Many of the country's leading scuba instructors have helped me select the best 100 dive sites covered in this book. These sites cover the length of the 185-mile (298 km) Belize Barrier Reef as well as the three offshore atoll reefs of Glovers, Turneffe and Lighthouse where the famous Great Blue Hole is located. For wreck divers I have added a chapter on Banco Chinchorro, a fourth atoll reef located just inside Mexican waters to the north, which can be reached from Belize.

The abundance and variety of marine life—including pelagics—is phenomenal in Belize, and I have indicated in the site descriptions what marine life is most likely to be encountered at a particular site.

Belize has many other attractions that I have touched on in this book: vast tracts of rain forest inhabited by beautiful butterflies, exotic birds and rare mammals such as the jaguar, jaguarundi and tapir. In addition, the numerous Maya ruins lying scattered in the jungle make fascinating side trips.

I have endeavored to ensure that all the information required by the visiting diver is contained within this single book, and I sincerely hope you find it both useful and informative.

Ned Middleton
Herne Bay
Kent, England
April 1994

CHAPTER I BELIZE

The Adventure Coast

Belize, formerly British Honduras, lies on the Caribbean coast of Central America. Bounded by Mexico to the north and Guatemala to the west and south, Belize is a country of 8,866 square miles (22,963 sq km) with a population of approximately 180,000. The northern half of the country is quite flat, with thick forests and swampland. The Maya and Cockscomb mountain ranges dominate the south which is also heavily forested, with high grasslands lying west of the mountains.

The Belize Barrier Reef, second only in size to the Great Barrier Reef of Australia, begins off the small Mexican town of Xcalak (ish-ka-lock), five miles (8 km) north of the Belize border, and extends for 185 miles (298 km) to its southern end near Hunting Caye. To the east of the barrier reef are three separate atoll reefs. There is also a fourth atoll reef just to the north in Mexican waters.

THE PAST

What is now Belize was once part of the Maya Empire, which flourished in the "Classic Period" from about A.D. 300 to about A.D. 900. By the latter part of the tenth century, Maya civilization was in abrupt decline, largely through internecine warfare and incursions by the fierce Toltecs from what is now western Mexico. In 1502, Columbus charted and named the Bay of Honduras, but he did not make landfall in what is now Belize. The European discovery of the area came in 1638 by shipwrecked sailors and buccaneers. By 1662, settlers from the British colony of Jamaica had established permanent colonies to exploit the rich forests of mahogany and other valuable timber. As this industry developed in the 18th century, English settlers were supplemented by Scottish and German traders and importations of African slaves to work the forests and what arable land there was.

Hostilities with the Spanish, who were already established in what are now Mexico and Guatemala, were frequent. The 1763 treaty of Paris, whereby the Spanish gave recognition to the English "Baymen," provided only a tenuous peace, and in 1779 the Spanish attacked what is now Belize City, driving out and decimating the population. By 1783 the Baymen had begun to reestablish themselves and were protected by treaties between England and Spain.

The Maya, meanwhile, had continually harrassed and attacked the settlers. In 1792 they attacked the British barracks at Orange Walk. They were repulsed and their leader, Marcus Canul, was mortally wounded. They never again posed a major threat. However, the Spanish launched another action in 1798, culminating in the battle of St. George's Caye, where they were turned back, ending their attempts at conquest of the area for good.

After the breakup of Spanish power in Central America, British sovereignty over Belize was recognized by Mexico with a treaty in 1826. Agreement on a common border with Guatemala was reached in 1859, though with some lingering dispute. In 1862, Belize was incorporated into the British colony of Jamaica, and became a separate colony called British Honduras in 1884.

A ministerial system of government was adopted in 1961, and in 1973 British Honduras changed its name to Belize. Independence from Britain was gained in 1981, but Belize maintains ties as a member of the Commonwealth.

A purple vase sponge provides a colorful niche for this goby as well as several brittle stars. Photo: Keith Ibsen.

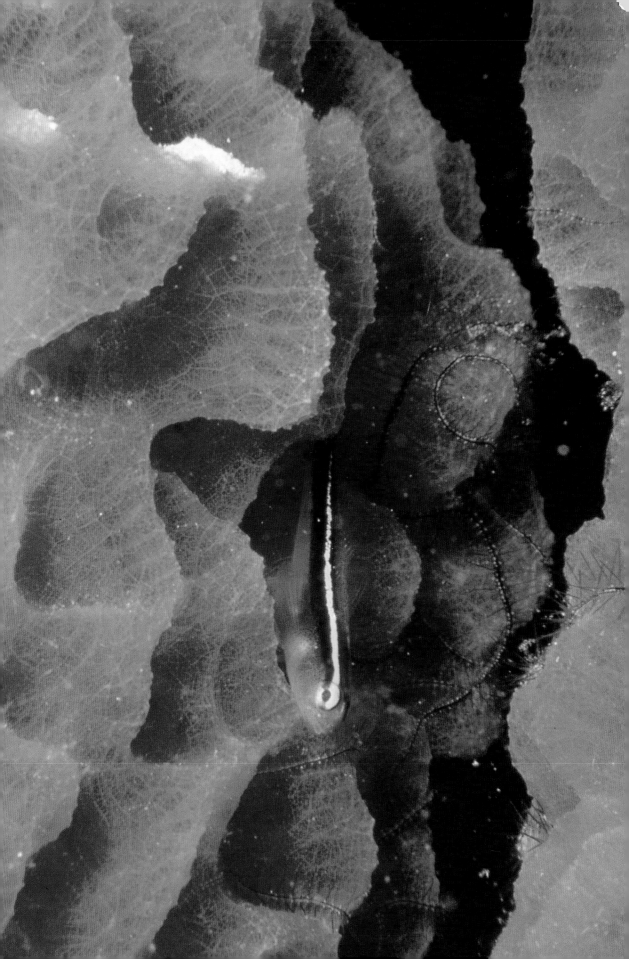

There are no high-rise buildings in Belize City, the former capital and largest city in Belize. Photo: Ned Middleton.

Youngsters in Belize, such as this Garifuna boy, learn about boats and the sea long before they learn about cars. Photo: Ned Middleton.

THE PRESENT

The population of Belize is representative of its history. About 40 percent of its people are Creole, a mixture of African and European. The Mestizo (Spanish and Amerindian) represent about 30 percent of the population. Other significant groups are the Garifuna (African and Amerindian), the Maya (pure descendants of the Mopan and Yucateca Maya), and the Anglos (European descendants and more recent arrivals from Europe and North America). There are also populations of East Indians, Chinese and Arabs.

There is a significant Mennonite community of Dutch and German origin in Belize which remains a mainstay of agricultural production. Always dressed in traditional fashion, the men are unmistakable in their denim bib-and-braces style overalls and straw hats, with shirts buttoned up to the neck. The ladies are equally conspicuous in their bonnets and long dresses. The Mennonites still favor horse-drawn farm equipment and carriages.

Situated at the mouth of the Belize River, Belize City is the largest center of population in the country, although it was supplanted as the capital in 1970 by the more centrally located Belmopan. Belize City is the hub of the country's lumber industry and has been a world leader in shipments of mahogany and logwood for hundreds of years. Despite this

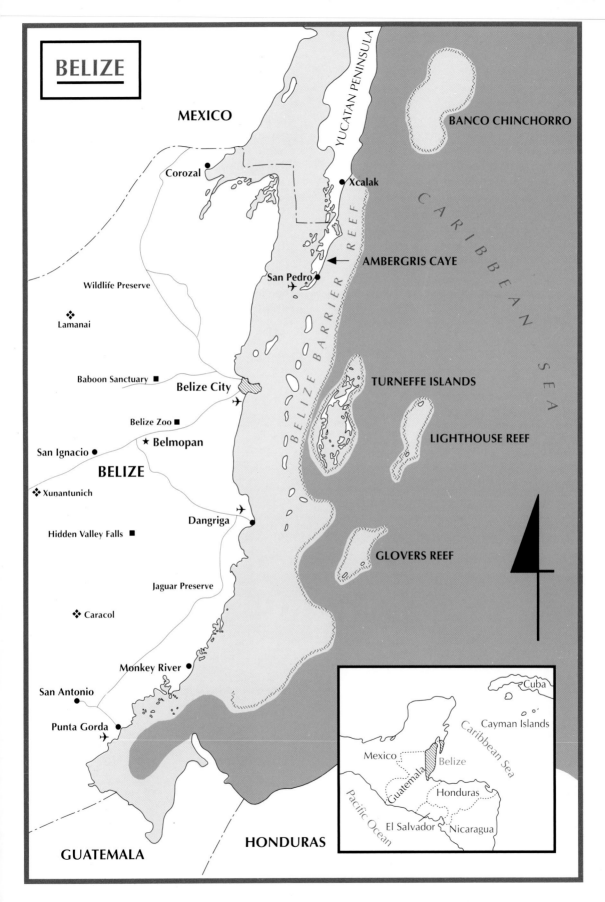

BELIZE

MEXICO

YUCATAN PENINSULA

BANCO CHINCHORRO

Corozal

Xcalak

CARIBBEAN SEA

AMBERGRIS CAYE

San Pedro

Wildlife Preserve

BELIZE BARRIER REEF

Lamanai

TURNEFFE ISLANDS

Baboon Sanctuary

Belize City

LIGHTHOUSE REEF

Belize Zoo

Belmopan

San Ignacio

BELIZE

Xunantunich

Hidden Valley Falls

Dangriga

GLOVERS REEF

Jaguar Preserve

Caracol

Monkey River

San Antonio

Punta Gorda

GUATEMALA

HONDURAS

Cuba

Cayman Islands

Caribbean Sea

Mexico

Belize

Guatemala

Honduras

Pacific Ocean

El Salvador

Nicaragua

13

statistic, the country as a whole is poor, and the city itself is a strange juxtaposition of modern banks, office buildings, shacks and old colonial buildings which hint of bygone wealth and elegance.

Although there has been a recent resurgence in demand for forest products, the sugar industry now accounts for over 50 percent of Belize's foreign exchange earnings, but efforts are being made to diversify agricultural production. Citrus products have the second largest share of exports, and bananas and cacao are also important crops. Commercial fishing supplies a number of North American markets, especially with lobster, conch, grouper and snapper. Since the organization of cooperatives in the 1960's, the fishing industry has managed to gain a considerable political voice.

Tourism is rapidly increasing in importance. Belize has much to offer the tourist: extensive Maya ruins, rain forests, exotic wildlife, beaches, sport fishing, and of course, scuba diving. San Pedro is the country's foremost center for tourism and is situated towards the southeast corner of Ambergris Caye. Streets of sand negotiated by tourists in golf carts keep a beachcomber feel amid the many modern hotels, resorts and shops. The beach here is sandy with numerous small jetties. The Belize Barrier Reef can clearly be seen less than one mile (1.6 k) out to sea. There are limited facilities for visiting yachts to tie up, but new jetties are under construction and being completed all the time. In the meantime, there is plenty of space to anchor a short distance from the shore. San Pedro is a twenty-minute ride by light aircraft from either the international airport or the municipal airport in Belize City.

Symbols of one of the country's main industries can be seen along the docks of Belize City where fishing nets dry in the sun. Photo: Ned Middleton.

USEFUL INFORMATION

Beaches. There are several miles of white sandy beaches on Ambergris Caye. Close to San Pedro, however, most of the beach is taken up by a number of essential jetties. The offshore atoll reefs provide an abundance of beaches and here it is easy to find an area that is entirely private. All beaches are generally clean and comprise a soft mixture of sand and crushed coral.

Climate. Summer temperatures usually range between 75-90°F (24-32°C), but are moderated by onshore winds, and it is rare for highs to exceed 95°F (35°C). The sun is extremely hot and you will need a blocker. In winter the temperatures vary from 60-80°F (16-27°C), but can be lower when the north winds blow.

The rainy season extends from July to January, and the remainder of the year is usually very dry. The hurricane season lasts from mid-summer through November, although Belize has not been adversely affected by a hurricane since 1978.

Mosquitoes and sand flies emerge in force in the late afternoon. Wearing slacks or long skirts, and long sleeves in the early evening, and applying a liberal amount of insect repellent will minimize the damage.

Currency. The Belize dollar (BZ$) has a fixed rate of exchange of BZ$2 to US$1, and such exchanges can be made at banks and most major hotels. United States dollars are accepted throughout the country for all goods and services. Be sure to retain sufficient United States (or other) funds for your return trip, as hotels may not have enough on hand when you need to convert back. Belize dollars are not easily exchanged at full value outside of the country. Most major credit cards and traveler's checks are widely accepted.

Electricity. The outlets in most hotels are 110 volts/60 cycles AC, as in the United States.

Entry and Exit Requirements. Passports are required, but no visa is necessary for citizens of the United States, United Kingdom and Commonwealth countries for a stay of up to one month. Visitors must have a round trip ticket issued in the country of origin. Customs clearance can be somewhat formal. Be sure to check with your travel agent for the latest information on import allowances. There is an airport departure tax of US$10.

Fishing. Belize offers world-class sport fishing, and charter boats with knowledgeable crews will help ensure that your fish stories will be real. The rivers and flats offer great tarpon, snook and bone fishing. Trolling and bottom fishing along the barrier reef and cayes, and farther offshore, regularly yield blue and white marlin, sailfish, tuna, barracuda, grouper, snapper, amberjack, mackerel, bonito, crevalle and many others.

Getting There. There are regularly scheduled direct flights from Miami, Los Angeles, New Orleans and Houston to Belize's international airport, a 20-minute drive from Belize City, about BZ$20 by taxi. New terminal buildings and a runway extension were completed in 1990 and the airport is now able to handle wide-bodied jets. If you are not flying direct to Belize but are changing flights in the United States, it is recommended that you recheck your luggage onto the connecting flight instead of checking it straight through.

All travel to either Ambergris Caye in the north or one of the many destinations in the south is usually undertaken by air. Four-wheel drive vehicles are available for rent at the international airport, but are quite expensive and are probably not cost effective unless you intend to keep moving.

There are four main highways which are normally in a good state of repair and never too busy. However, the roads within Belize City and as far as the international airport are generally in poor condition. Off the highways and away from Belize City and Belmopan, the roads are dirt tracks, making four-wheel drive vehicles essential. It can take up to seven hours to drive from Belize City to Punta Gorda. The highways are: Northern Highway—Belize City to Corozal; Western Highway—Belize City to Belmopan, San Ignacio and the Guatemalan border; Hummingbird Highway—Belmopan to Dangriga; Southern Highway—Dangriga to Punta Gorda.

Maya Airways and Tropic Air are the main internal carriers but new airlines such as Island Air are opening up for business. These airlines meet all incoming international flights and also operate out of the municipal airport in Belize City. The aircraft are small single-engine Cessna or larger twin-engine Otter or

Islander which can carry up to 20 passengers.

Be sure to confirm your return trip well in advance and then again the day before you intend to depart.

Language. English, the official language, is spoken by over half the population and is prevalent in all major tourist destinations. Nearly a third of Belizeans speak Spanish, and in some areas of the country such as the Corazal and Orange Walk districts in the north, and the Cayo district in the south, it is the first language. Garifuna and Maya are heard in the southern districts of Stann Creek and Toledo. Nearly everyone throughout Belize speaks Creole, an English dialect. Radio Belize One broadcasts about 80 percent of its programs in English.

Photography. Island Photos in San Pedro, run by Joe Miller, has a full range of Nikonos and other underwater cameras and strobes available for rent at reasonable rates. Joe also has a number of underwater video systems.

In addition to repairs and servicing, Joe provides film processing. Films are processed overnight for both color prints and color slides (E-6). Friendly advice is always available for free, and more detailed instruction, including a customized underwater course tailored to your special needs, can be arranged.

While Island Photos is a reliable, full-service shop, repair facilities are few and far between elsewhere in the country. You should bring plenty of film and batteries, since the ones in Belize are often sold after a long shelf life.

It's a good idea to prepare a typed list of all your camera equipment with serial numbers. Deposit this with customs officials when you leave your home country. Keep a copy of the list and have it ready when you return home.

Shopping. Belize is not a shopping mecca, but there are many small shops that sell native crafts and clothing from Mexico and Guatemala. For conservation reasons, souvenirs made from anything taken from the sea should be avoided, especially items made from black coral and the shell of the hawksbill turtle, which is an endangered species.

My favorite souvenirs are the carvings in Zericote wood. I have looked at many of these carvings, and what I believe to be the best are those carved by Roy Rivers and offered by

The sandy streets of San Pedro add to the beachcomber atmosphere of this tourist center. Photo: Ned Middleton.

Small wooden jetties dot the beaches of San Pedro on Ambergris Caye. The Belize Barrier Reef comes closest to shore here and there is excellent diving only a short skiff-ride offshore. Photo: Ned Middleton.

Lionel Vasquez (53 King St., Belize City). I like his renditions of the cormorant (known locally as the loon), which looks as though it is going to dip under the waves at any moment, but his dolphins, sharks and other carvings are also very good.

Sightseeing. There are Maya ruins scattered throughout Belize. **Altun Ha** (Water of the Rock) is the most extensively excavated ruin in all of Belize, and is about 30 miles (48 km) north of Belize City. Here was discovered what is believed to be the largest Maya jade carving in existence, a portrayal of the head of Kinisch Ahau, the Maya Sun God. The Temple of the Green Tomb, which contained, in addition to human remains, a spectacular collection of jade carvings and jewelry, was also uncovered here. Altun Ha dates from about A.D. 600,

within the Classic Period of the Maya, although the site itself is believed to have been first settled over 2,000 years ago.

Xunantunich (The Maiden of the Rock) is about 80 miles (129 km) west of Belize City, on the Mopan River, and can only be reached by ferry from San Jose Succotz. The temple sits atop a carved limestone ridge, about 600 feet (182 m) above sea level, from which the main pyramid rises another 130 feet (39 m), offering a dazzling view of Belize and Guatemala. This site has also been extensively excavated and most of the architecture dates from the 7th to 10th centuries.

To the north, and a little farther west than Altun Ha, the magnificent ruins of **Lamanai** (Submerged Crocodile) rise from the jungle. It is a large complex and can be reached by river

Sea anemones add to the myriad of colors found in Belize's underwater landscape. Photo: Keith Ibsen.

A resting hummingbird is a rare sight. They can usually be seen in the late afternoon flitting among the hibiscus blooms. Photo: Ned Middleton.

Divers with a sharp eye may be treated to rare sightings such as this wing oyster clinging tightly to a sea rod. Photo: Ned Middleton.

boat, or by a four-wheel drive vehicle in the dry season. There is still much excavation remaining to be done; nonetheless, there is much to see, and the sight of these elaborate structures looming out of the jungle is striking.

The tallest man-made structure in all of Belize is the **Canaa** (Sky Palace), the great pyramid at **Caracol**. Although first discovered in 1938, it is only recently that the true scale and importance of the site has become known. Indeed, there is evidence that Caracol may, at one time in the middle Classic Period, have been the "supreme" Maya city. South of San Ignacio, Caracol is not easily reached, but arrangements can be made with tour operators.

There are many other worthwhile Maya sites in Belize. Information about these is readily available in Belize or through the Belize Tourist Board in the United States (see Appendix 2).

There are natural wonders in Belize as well. **Mountain Pine Ridge** is about 70 miles (113 km) west of Belize City, not far from Xunantunich. This national forest reserve has thousands of acres of pine forests, mountain streams, river valleys, and abundant and exotic wildlife. Nature trips and trail rides are available. The noted **Hidden Valley Falls** plunges over 1,000 feet (303 m) to the valley floor.

The **Cockscomb Basin Jaguar Preserve**, about 20 miles (32 km) south of Dangriga, is 150 square miles (389 sq km) of rain forest and high jungle set aside for the protection of the spotted jaguar, the largest wild cat in the Americas. This preserve is also home to the puma, ocelot, jaguarundi, peccary, anteater, armadillo, margay, brocket deer, agoti, paca and the Baird's tapir, the national animal of Belize, which can weigh as much as 600 pounds (272 kg).

Crooked Tree Wildlife Sanctuary, 33 miles (53 km) northwest of Belize City, features lagoons, swamps and waterways that are home to a rich diversity of birdlife including white pelicans, ospreys, herons, hummingbirds, toucans, ibis, sea eagles, grebes, kites, kingfishers, vultures, egrets and the Jabiru stork, the largest flying bird in the Western Hemisphere, with a wingspan of up to 12 feet (3.6 m). Coatimundi, crocodiles, iguanas, turtles and black howler monkeys are some of the wildlife that also may be seen here.

Black howler monkeys, an endangered species, also have their "own" preserve at Bermudian Landing, the **Community Baboon Sanctuary**. Landowners in this 18 square mile area (47 sq km) cooperate in the protection of these monkeys, known locally as "baboons."

The **Belize Zoo**, at mile 30 (48 km) on Western Highway, houses an exotic collection of native species, a number of which are endangered. The zoo is well into the process of modernizing and is the center of a national environmental education program.

Also endangered and protected is the **manatee**, a gentle sea-dwelling mammal. This friendly creature can be found in the Belize River upstream from the city and in the mangrove-covered cayes which dominate the scenery between the mainland and the reef.

Orchid fanciers can arrange special trips on the jungle rivers and in the rain forests, tailored to spot a large number of the more than 250 varieties of orchid found in Belize.

There are several cave systems open to visitors, among them the **Rio Frio Caves** near Augustine Village. The largest cavern is a showcase of stalactites, crystalline flowstone and other geological wonders, and like many caves in Belize, shows evidence of a Maya past.

Time. Belize is in the Central Time zone and does not observe Daylight Savings Time.

Water. Belize has water-table aquifers and artesian aquifers. The former are shallow and are used for water supplies throughout the country. The quality is generally good and the country has sufficient potable water for the foreseeable future. Bottled water is widely available throughout the country and is recommended for all visitors.

CHAPTER **II** ACCOMMODATIONS

In Belize there is a hotel to suit every pocket. The more remote ones out of town are usually more expensive.

With the notable exception of the offshore resorts, few hotels run their own diving facility. However, at the time of publication, all the hotels listed here either have a dive shop or have arrangements with one of the local dive shops to provide scuba. Be sure to confirm diving arrangements when making your reservations to avoid additional costs.

Hotels in Belize have a 3-tier pricing structure:

Budget: Up to US$25 per night.
Moderate: US$26 to US$50 per night.
Expensive: Over US$50 per night.

The feather duster, like its kin, the Christmas tree worm, uses its delicate "feathers" as filters to remove food from the surrounding water. Photo: Keith Ibsen.

The cabanas at Ramon's Village blend gracefully into the scenery and provide a truly tropical ambiance for guests. Photo: Ned Middleton.

	Rooms/Units	Price Range	Credit Cards	Air Conditioning	Restaurant	Pool	Beach	Fishing
Belize City & District								
Belcove Hotel Tel: 02-73054	5	B						■
Radisson Ft. George Tel: 02-33333	100	E	■	■	■	■		■
Ramada Royal Reef Tel: 02-32670	118	E	■	■	■	■		■
The Shores Tel: 021-2023	4	M-E	■		■		■	■
Ambergris Caye								
Alijua Suites Tel: 026-2791	6	E	■	■				■
Barrier Reef Hotel Tel: 026-2075	11	M-E	■	■	■	■	■	■
Belize Yacht Club Tel: 026-2567	55	E	■	■	■	■		■
Belizean Reef Suites Tel: 026-2582	5	E		■			■	■
Capricorn Resort Tel: 026-2809	4	E			■		■	
Captain Morgan's Retreat Tel: 026-2567	21	E	■		■	■	■	
Caribbean Villas Tel: 026-2715	10	E	■	■		■	■	■
Casa Blanca Hotel Tel: 026-2924	5	M-E	■	■	■			
Casa Caracol Tel: 026-3077	2	E	■				■	■

	Rooms/Units	Price Range	Credit Cards	Air Conditioning	Restaurant	Pool	Beach	Fishing
Chateau Caribe Tel: 026-3233	6	E	■	■		■	■	■
Coconuts Carib. Hotel Tel: 026-3500	12	E	■	■			■	■
Conch Shell Hotel Tel: 026-2062	10	M-E	■				■	■
Coral Beach Hotel Tel: 026-2013	19	M	■	■	■		■	■
Corona Del Mar Tel: 026-2055	4	E	■	■			■	■
El Pescador Lodge Tel: 026-2398	13	E	■				■	■
The Green Parrot Tel: 026-2331	6	M			■		■	■
Hideaway Sports Lodge Tel: 026-2141	19	M-E	■	■	■	■	■	
Hotel Playador Tel: 026-2870	20	E	■	■	■		■	■
Journey's End Hotel Tel: 026-2173	71	E	■	■	■	■	■	■
Mosquito Coast Villas Tel: 026-3077	2	E		■		■		■
Paradise Condominiums Tel: 026-3077	20	E		■		■	■	■
Paradise Resort Hotel Tel: 026-2083	27	E	■	■	■		■	■
Ramon's Village Tel: 026-2071	60	E	■	■	■	■	■	■

	Rooms/Units	Price Range	Credit Cards	Air Conditioning	Restaurant	Pool	Beach	Fishing
Rock's Inn Tel: 026-2326	14	E	■	■			■	■
Royal Palm Villas Tel: 026-2148	20	E	■	■		■	■	■
San Pedro Holiday Hotel Tel: 026-2014	17	E	■	■	■		■	■
Sands Hotel Tel: 026-2510	7	M-E		■				■
Seven Seas Hotel Tel: 026-2382	12	E	■				■	■
Sun Breeze Beach Hotel Tel: 026-2191	39	E	■	■	■		■	
Tres Cocos Houses Tel: 026-3077	6	E					■	■
Offshore								
Blackbird Resort Turneffe Islands Tel: 02-32772	11	B	■		■		■	■
Blue Horizon Northeast Caye Tel: 05-22294	2	M					■	■
Blue Marlin Lodge South Water Caye Tel: 05-22243	15	M-E	■	■	■		■	■
Cottage Colony St. George's Caye Tel: 02-12020	14	E	■	■	■		■	■
Glover's Atoll Resort Glover's Reef Tel: 05-23048	6	B			■		■	■

The spectacular scenery along the drop-off on the eastern side of the Turneffe Islands is a special treat for divers. Photo: Keith Ibsen.

	Rooms/Units	Price Range	Credit Cards	Air Conditioning	Restaurant	Pool	Beach	Fishing
Island Camps Tobacco Caye Tel: 05-23433	9	B-M			■		■	■
Jiminez Caban Caye Caulker Tel: 022-2175	6	B-M						■
Leslie's Cottages South Water Caye Tel: 05-22119	10	E			■		■	■
Lena's Hotel Caye Caulker Tel: 02-22106	19	M					■	■
Lighthouse Reef Resort Lighthouse Reef Tel: 02-31205	11	E	■	■	■		■	■
Lorna's Guesthouse Tobacco Caye Tel: 05-22119	3	B					■	■
Manta Reef Resort Glover's Reef Tel: 02-31895	12	B-M	■		■			■
Ocean's Edge Lodge Tobacco Caye Tel: 05-22294	5	M-E			■		■	■
Rendezvous Cay Resort Rendezvous Caye Tel: 02-72297	5	B					■	■
Ricardo's Beach Huts Bluefield Range Tel: 02-31609	11	B					■	■
Spanish Bay Resort Spanish Lookout Caye Tel: 02-77288	10	E			■		■	■

	Rooms/Units	Price Range	Credit Cards	Air Conditioning	Restaurant	Pool	Beach	Fishing
St. George's Island Cott. St. George's Caye Tel: 02-44190	6	E			■		■	■
St. George's Island Lodge St. George's Caye Tel: 02-12121	9	E			■		■	■
The Wave Hotel Gallows Point Tel: 02-73054	6	M			■			■
Turneffe Flats Lodge Turneffe Islands Tel: 01-49564	12	E	■				■	■
Turneffe Island Lodge Turneffe Islands Tel: 02-30236	13	E			■		■	■
Whipray Caye Lodge Whipray Caye Tel: 06-23130	8	B						■
Stann Creek District								
Amazing Grace Tel: 06-22436	4	-			■		■	■
Caribbean View Hotel Tel: 05-22803	9	B				■		
Isolene's Guesthouse Tel: 05-22006	7	B			■			
Jaguar Reef Lodge Tel: 06-22027	14	E	■		■		■	■
Nautical Inn Tel: 06-22310	12	E	■	■	■		■	■
Placencia Lagoon Resort Tel: 06-22363		M-E	■		■		■	■

CHAPTER III DINING

These comments on the flavor of Belize cuisine are based on my own gastronomical forays into the restaurants of San Pedro.

Belize food is simple yet enticing. One of the most popular national dishes is called "rice and peas." It consists of white rice, peas, chicken and a side salad. Nothing very exciting—until, that is, you taste it. The chicken is cooked in a very tasty sauce and the entire meal is both filling and enjoyable.

Belizeans do not usually eat mutton, and beef is an expensive import. Chicken and fish, therefore, form a large part of the staple diet with different restauranteurs putting their own particular stamp on each dish. Tourists should not confine themselves to eating in their own hotel. For variety, try some of the other hotels or, better still, try some of my own favorite eating houses in San Pedro.

Celi's

Dinner at Celi's is an enjoyable experience not to be overlooked. They have freshly baked bread, and specialize in seafood and homestyle American fare. The house specialty is shrimp *deJonghe*, which is shrimp cooked in garlic butter and herbs, and served over steamed rice. Wine and beer are available.

The Coffee Shop

Right next to the San Pedro airstrip is The Coffee Shop run by the delightful Janis Morin who claims to put out "The best breakfast in town with a Mexican flair." They are open from 6 A.M. to 3 P.M. and primarily serve breakfast, snacks and light lunches.

Elvi's Kitchen

The menu at this popular restaurant, which is always busy at midday and in the evening, favors seafood dishes. However, there is also a selection of chicken and steak dishes as well as burgers and club sandwiches. At this central location on Pescador Drive, the shrimp combo with wine and cheese is highly recommended.

Jade Garden

For the very best Catonese cuisine and excellent fresh seafood dishes served in a relaxed family atmosphere, try the Jade Garden. This is one of my favorite eating places for dinner and the Chinese dishes are equal to any I've experienced, including those in Hong Kong. It is located just south of the airstrip and is only a short stroll or taxi ride from town. Full bar facilities are available.

Lily's

Hidden away in the middle of San Pedro just off Carbeña Street is this jewel of a restaurant run by the charming Lily Paz. The house specialty is a seafood combo. The menu includes seafood, chicken and steak dishes.

San Pedro Grill

With the motto of "No shirt—No shoes—No problem" the San Pedro Grill, run by the delightful Stella Worthington, is an excellent place for an early breakfast or lunch. Their specialties are seafood and barbecue dishes, and their prices are very competitive. They are centrally situated at Fido's Court and open from 6 A.M. to 6 P.M. Separate bar facilities are available in Fido's Court.

Named for the orange balls at the tips of each tentacle that surrounds its mouth, the orange-balled anemone can be seen in full display only at night when it is feeding. Photo: Keith Ibsen.

CHAPTER IV   DIVING

There is a great variety of reef types and diving experiences in Belize. The Barrier Reef is 185 meandering miles (298 km) of unspoiled beauty. It varies from 8 to 16 miles (13-26 km) from the mainland to less than one mile (1.6 km) offshore from Ambergris Caye. Much of it is totally unexplored and all of it is easily accessible by boat. The reef is like a gigantic wall running parallel to the coast. Between the mainland and the reef are shallow, sandy waters with numerous mangrove-covered islands (cayes).

To the east of the Barrier Reef are three separate atoll reefs. There is also a fourth atoll reef, Banco Chinchorro, just to the north in Mexican waters, which will be of particular interest to wreck divers.

The three Belize atoll reefs are formed on two tiers of submarine ridges: Turneffe and Glover's on one ridge and Lighthouse on a separate ridge farther to the east. This accounts for their similar outlines and NE-SW orientations. Deep marine trenches separate the two ridges.

While much of the flora and fauna is similar throughout the reef system, there are individual differences to be found everywhere. A particular type of fish may be seen on almost every dive, but during mating season it may congregate in only one or two areas in great numbers. Hard corals, gorgonians, sea fans, tunicates, and shellfish of amazing variety populate Belize coastal waters, but the predominance of one in a particular stretch of reef may give that area its name. Similarly, there are areas where grouper are known to shoal, others where large stingray are prolific or where the diver may encounter a whale shark. The manta ray and spotted eagle ray are fairly common, and the diver can reasonably expect to see one of these magnificent creatures during his visit. Hammerhead shark, Caribbean reef shark and even the oceanic white tip shark are seen occasionally, but these lucky sightings are rare.

CONSERVATION

A well-known British politician once said, "We have not inherited the sea from our parents, we have borrowed it from our children."

Our very existence, the future of life as we know it, rests on the successful conservation of the sea and its creatures. The sea cannot continue to dilute pollution forever, so we must not add to this problem by thoughtless behavior. In the same way, the coral reef cannot stand a constant barrage of damage from anchors and divers forever.

Few appreciate the sea and its life as much as divers, and it is our responsibility to minimize any impact divers' excursions may have. Below are a few simple guidelines to help prevent damage to the marine environment:

- Do not throw any non-biodegradables into the ocean.
- If you see trash on the sea floor, bring it up.
- Anchor only on sandy patches to avoid breaking coral which has taken hundreds of years to grow.
- Practice good neutral buoyancy to keep from banging into the reef and thus inadvertently causing damage to coral.
- Secure any dangling straps and be conscious of where your fins are.

The queen angelfish is the most colorful of the seven species of angelfishes and is frequently seen in Belize. Photo: Keith Ibsen.

Large sponges protrude at right angles along the incredible drop-off of Half Moon Wall on Lighthouse Reef. Photo: Joe Miller.

- If your neutral buoyancy skills are weak, take a refresher before diving the reef.
- Divers without gloves will be less inclined to touch marine life. Set a good example for other divers and leave your dive gloves in your equipment bag.
- Divers should not remove any living creature from the sea including shells, shellfish, fish and coral.
- Do not buy jewelry or souvenirs made from turtle shells. It is illegal to bring them into the United States.

DIVE FLAGS

When divers are actively diving from a boat, a dive flag should be raised. A rigid flag or one held open by a stiff wire is preferred to a cloth flag which can only be viewed on a windy day. Two patterns of dive flag will be seen in Belize. The most common is the red and white flag used in the United States. Occasionally the international blue and white "A" flag will also be seen. Both flags have the same meaning: "I have divers down. Keep well clear at slow speed."

EQUIPMENT

While many dive operations can supply quality dive gear, it is highly recommended that certified divers bring their own gear with the exception of tanks and weights. Remember to bring backups if you have them. It might save you a frustrating trip hunting around for a replacement part, such as a hose or a low pressure BC connector for your particular type of equipment.

Some operations can only supply tanks and weight belts with weights. If you are concerned about equipment, check with your hotel or resort on availability and brand names before you arrive.

OFFSHORE RESORTS

These are "up market" resorts on the three major offshore atolls that cater to the dedicated diver. Although more expensive, the facilities are impressive and the diving almost unlimited. The only drawback is one will get to see little of Belize and meet very few local people.

SHIPWRECKS

Unlike the Mexican atoll Banco Chinchorro to the north, Belize itself has little to offer the ardent wreck diver. There is the *Sayonara* off Caye Bokel, the wreck of either a tug or a trawler off Hunting Caye, and two wrecks on Lighthouse Reef. Just about all other wrecked ships are sitting high and dry on top of the reefs. This is ironic because ships have been wrecked all along this coast for many years. Gold coins from Spanish galleons continue to come to light. Though remotely possible, it is unlikely that the visiting diver will find anything of immense value and, in any event, all such finds are the property of the Belize government and are to be reported.

Many ancient cannon and ship fittings are on display throughout the country especially in San Pedro. Each individual item is part of the country's maritime history and one day, when Belize can afford to invest money into researching its past, each one of these artifacts will become an important link in the chain of events which created a country.

TYPICAL DIVE TRIP

Diving trips are as varied as the hotel they are booked out of. The diver can visit the reef by skiff and be back in time for a light lunch before repeating the process in the afternoon. Some operations have larger boats that run 2- or 3-day offshore trips with 10 to 20 divers.

A typical two-day offshore trip would have a program something like this:

Day One

6:30 A.M.	Depart San Pedro
9:00 A.M.	Dive northern Turneffe Islands
3:00 P.M.	Dive Lighthouse Reef
Night	On Half Moon Caye with a bar-b-que and visit to the bird sanctuary.

Day Two

7:00 A.M.	Depart Half Moon Caye
9:00 A.M.	Dive the Great Blue Hole
3:00 P.M.	Dive northern Turneffe Islands (different site)
4:30 P.M.	Arrive San Pedro

The Belize Aggressor and other live-aboard boats offer almost unlimited diving and can reach all of the atoll reefs. Photo: Keith Ibsen.

Tube sponges adorn the reefs throughout Belize. Photo: Ned Middleton.

Many dive shops are located along the beach front of San Pedro and offer a variety of dive options. Divers can book a one-tank morning or afternoon dive to a nearby reef, or an overnight trip to offshore sites. Photo: Ned Middleton.

The octopus is one of the camouflage experts of the reef. It has the ability to quickly change colors to match the surrounding terrain. Photo: Joe Miller.

Tides, Waves and Wind

Diving is generally conducted without any reference to the tide as the average range is only about 1 to 1-1/2 feet (31- 46 cm). When the north winds really blow, this can be in excess of 2 feet (62 cm). Of course, hurricanes and other tropical storms can cause tidal extremes. Currents are usually negligible.

The wind is mostly steady from the northeast at 5 to 15 knots, except in the south where southeast winds are frequent. The northeast winds generate large Caribbean swells which can make diving difficult on exposed shores.

While wave action inside the reef or on the sheltered side of atolls is minimal, divers must still be cautious of the surge when close to the reef and near the surface.

The sea breaking over the reef crest allows the skipper of a boat to see the extent of the reef. On those occasions when the sea is flat calm, an additional hazard is present for small boats as the edge of the reef becomes hard to define.

Topography

Blue holes, as they are known throughout the Caribbean, are common in several countries, but the largest one of all is right in the center of Lighthouse Reef and is known as The Great Blue Hole. Formed in the limestone substrata, they are officially called "karst-eroded sinkholes" and were created prior to the melting which ended the Great Ice Age, when sea levels were much lower than today. Caves, caverns, tunnels, stalactites and stalagmites are common along the entire Belize shelf.

Explanations for some of the more common topography are listed below.

Caye. A caye is an island of sand and/or mangrove which is a permanent feature above the surface, but is not a reef crest.

Coral. The conditions for coral growth and the long term development of the reef are considered near perfect in Belize. Clear water, sunlight, water temperature, a firm substrate, salinity levels and the constant circulation of well-oxygenated water all play a vital role in the process.

While the corals are typical of the Caribbean they tend to be especially well developed. There are many varieties of corals, but the major reef-building ones are the massive forms of brain coral; various types of finger coral; two well-known branching corals, elkhorn and staghorn; and sheet coral.

Cut. A navigable gap between two reef crests.

Patch Reef. These are small clumps of coral heads on a shallow sandy bottom. They are particularly common inside Glover's and Lighthouse Reefs and at the southern end of the barrier reef. In most cases they are too shallow for scuba diving, but are excellent places to snorkel.

Reef Crest. Underwater the barrier reef or any of the atoll reefs are a single entity, although at the surface they appear broken. That part of the reef which reaches the surface is the reef crest and each of these has an individual name, often adopted from the nearest caye.

Reef Wall. Both the barrier reefs and the atoll reefs fall away vertically into the abyss. This reef wall or drop-off is most dramatic when it faces east.

Visibility

Many of the natural circumstances which contrive to reduce underwater visibility do not exist in Belize. It is because the reef is between 8 to 16 miles (13-26 km) offshore (except at Ambergris Caye) that it is not affected by river outflow and rainfall washing off the land. In addition, the strong currents created by large tidal ranges are non-existent in the Caribbean. With very few exceptions, such as diving close to mangroves, the underwater visibility is always at its maximum for anywhere in the world—165 feet (50 m). Beyond this distance the water is simply blue. The effects of storms elsewhere in the Caribbean can, however, reduce the visibility to between 65 feet (20 m) and 100 feet (30 m).

Water Temperature

The water temperature is fairly constant throughout the year and is generally in the mid to high 70'sF (23-26^{0}C), but can reach the low 80'sF (26-28 ^{0}C). A lightweight lycra body suit, more for protection from coral abrasions than for warmth, is a good solution. For those needing more thermal protection a 1/16th inch (4 mm) suit should be adequate.

CHAPTER **V**   **THE BELIZE BARRIER REEF**

A large and complicated system of individual reefs extends from the Yucatan Peninsula to South America. The largest of these reefs is the Belize Barrier Reef. Not only is this the largest single reef in the Caribbean; it is also the largest reef in both the northern and western hemispheres. In fact it is second only in size to the Great Barrier Reef of Australia.

The Belize Barrier Reef actually begins at a point 5 miles (8 km) north of Belize near the small Mexican town of Xcalak. The reef then stretches south for 185 miles (298 km) before coming to an end near Hunting Caye.

The reef is like a gigantic wall running parallel to the coast. The distance from the reef to the mainland varies from 8 to 16 miles (13-26 km), but is much closer at the northern portion off Ambergris Caye where it is clearly seen from the shore. Between the mainland and the reef are shallow sandy waters with numerous mangrove-covered islands (cayes).

AMBERGRIS CAYE TO STINGRAY FLATS
(Panel Map One)

Along the entire length of **Ambergris Caye** the reef is comprised of spectacular three-dimensional coral formations which include canyons, grottoes and tunnels. Curiously, the more common reef fishes do not appear here in great numbers compared to elsewhere. However, there are a greater number of pelagic fish such as sharks and rays. There are also a considerable number of porpoise and turtle to be seen.

This entire northern stretch of reef is ideal for macro photography. Vase sponges, tube sponges and coral pinnacles are home for countless miniscule creatures awaiting discovery. Shrimps, brittle stars, nudibranchs, tube worms and tunicates of every imaginable color are often overlooked by the diver. My particular favorite is the red-banded coral shrimp. These are present on almost every dive and are usually found along ledges and gullies, or on the ceilings of swim-throughs and overhangs in the shallower stretches of coral. Without touching them, they are easily coaxed out into a suitable position for a photograph.

Inside the reef, the water is murky and sandy. The busy surface traffic makes snorkeling both impractical and dangerous. However, once you reach the reef it fills your vision: shallow, well-lit water with a myriad of corals and fishes in bright iridescent colors.

Just to the north of **Reef Point** are **Conch Flats [1]**, large sandy areas inside the reef covered in sea grass—not ideal for diving as it soon becomes boring. Sea grass is, however, the staple diet of both the conch and the turtle, and is therefore an important part of the ecosystem.

For the game fisherman, this is a spot to catch wahoo, a large silver fish which puts up a good fight. It is also a good fish for eating. These fish are rarely seen by divers.

On the seaward side of the reef, the coral drops down to a ledge which, in places, can be up to half a mile (.8 km) wide before it drops off into the deep blue waters of the Caribbean. Here pelagics abound. Although they are predominantly solitary creatures, as many as five whale sharks, all 25-30 feet (8-9 m) long have been seen together here. They were most likely feeding on the plankton which was being blown offshore by the prevailing wind at the time they were sighted.

Along Ambergris Caye, nurse sharks are probably more common than elsewhere in Belize. Most often they are found sitting on the

The green moray is the largest of all Atlantic morays and can grow to lengths of over six feet (2 m). Photo: Keith Ibsen.

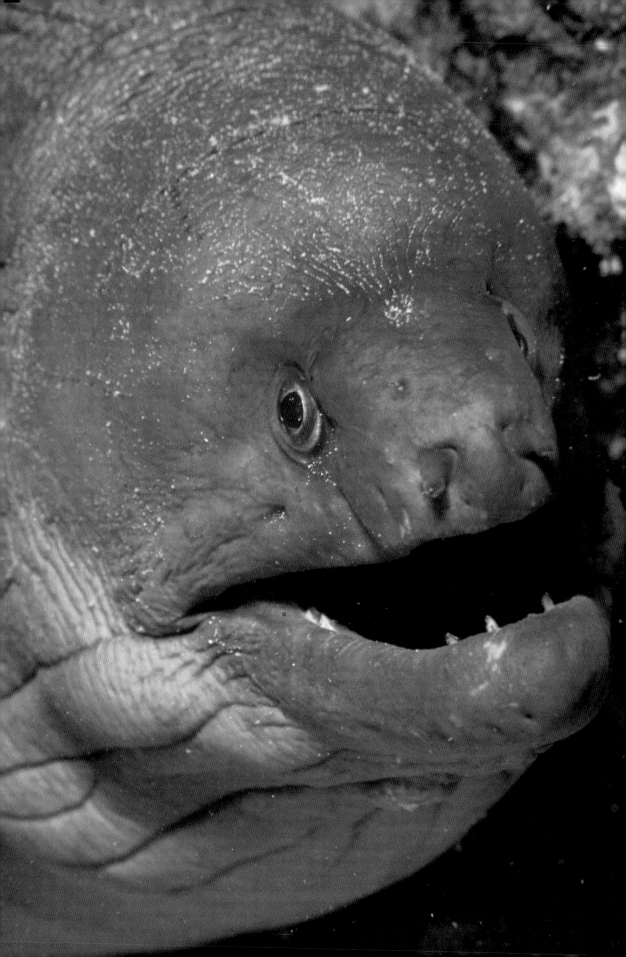

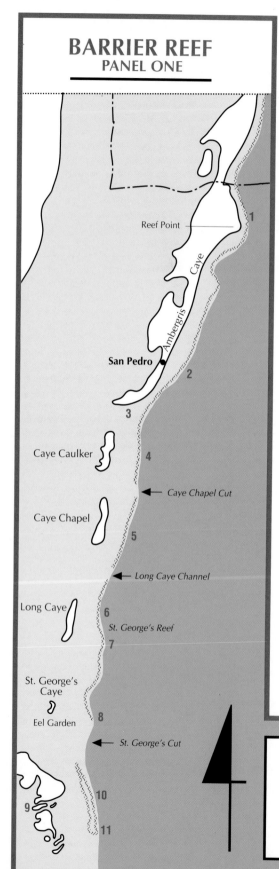

BARRIER REEF
PANEL ONE

Reef Point

Ambergris Caye

San Pedro

Caye Caulker

Caye Chapel Cut

Caye Chapel

Long Caye Channel

Long Caye

St. George's Reef

St. George's
Caye

Eel Garden

St. George's Cut

1. Conch Flats
2. Tuffy Cut
3. Hol Chan Marine
   Reserve
4. Caye Caulker Reef
5. Chapel Reef
6. Ski Slopes
7. Turtle Leap
8. The Wall
9. Drowned Cayes
10. Gallows Point Reef
11. Stingray Flats

seabed amongst the gullies and grottoes. Occasionally one can be seen swimming along the reef, but it will quickly disappear when it sees a diver. It is a harmless shark provided it is left unmolested. But be forewarned: the nurse shark is a stubborn creature and if it bites, it has a reputation for not letting go!

The reef immediately east of **San Pedro**, the main town on Ambergris Caye, is well known for its great variety of coral. **Tuffy Cut [2]** is a prime example of this. Staghorn, elkhorn, brain and lettuce coral are all here in abundance, as are gorgonian sea fans of pale green, deep purple and red that add to the riot of colors and shapes.

Off the southern tip of Ambergris Caye is the **Hol Chan Marine Reserve [3]**. Hol Chan is Mayan for "little channel." This sanctuary was officially established in 1987, and since then the return of all species of fish has been quite dramatic. The reserve covers approximately three square miles (7.8 sq km) and is divided into three zones. Each one is clearly marked by buoys. The entire reserve focuses on a cut through the reef which is little more than 25 yards (23 m) wide and 30 feet (9 m) deep.

Zone A includes the reef and is covered with almost every type of coral found in the Caribbean. Here there are plenty of grouper, but it is the green moray eel, found in the small caves alongside the wall of the channel, which really catch the eye. The morays have become used to divers and are often hand-fed, which sometimes has led to some careless divers being inadvertently bitten when fingers and food were indistinguishable to the moray. Feeding the morays and fish in general is also controversial because as the fish come to expect handouts, they cease to hunt for themselves.

Zone B is an area of sea grass where turtle, conch and even the remarkable little sea horse are found. Spotted eagle rays and stingrays of

The eye of a conch peers out from its shell. Conch Flats is a sandy site covered with sea grass, a staple food of the conch. Photo: Keith Ibsen.

all but the largest sizes are also here. There is a little-known blue hole called the **Boca Ciega Blue Hole** in this zone. This sinkhole, which opens into a larger cavern, is dangerous and not recommended for diving.

   Zone C comprises the mangroves. These are a feature of almost all the cayes found inside the reef. They provide a home for a large population of juvenile fishes which remain in the safety of the networks of mangrove roots and trunks until they are large enough to survive in open water. Indeed, the entire marine reserve is a fine example of three completely different areas which are interdependent. Creatures from both the mangroves and the reef feed on the sea grass. The reef receives nutrients from both the other areas. Minute organisms originating in the mangroves may be blown offshore and become part of the plankton which attracts such pelagics as the manta ray and the whale shark.

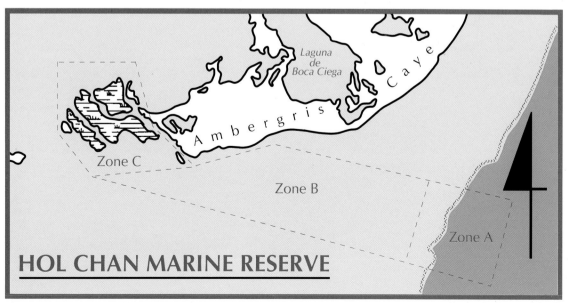

HOL CHAN MARINE RESERVE

South of Ambergris Caye the reefs which break the surface take their names from nearby cayes. The mainland is now 13 to 14 miles (21-23 km) to the west, and in between is a vast area of shallow water with numerous cayes of sand and mangroves.

Underwater, **Caye Caulker Reef [4]** (also Corker) and **Chapel Reef [5]** display large coral outcrops punctuated with gaps of varying widths. The coral outcrops are like cliff faces whereas the gaps are gentle, sandy slopes. These are termed "spur and groove" formations. In some places the narrower gaps have become tunnels as the coral has grown across the gap. All along these reefs spiny lobster can be found inside carefully selected hideaways.

Caye Chapel Cut is a navigable entrance through Chapel Reef, but it should only be attempted by those familiar with its hazards. By comparison, **Long Caye Channel** is a much larger and safer channel between Chapel Reef and **St. George's Reef**.

The northern one-third of St. George's Reef is known as the **Ski Slopes [6]** on account of the spur and groove structures. The sandy slopes stretch down from the shallows all the way to the reef wall. This area is not particularly popular as the remainder of the reef is much more vibrant and colorful.

Farther south along St. George's Reef is a spot called **Turtle Leap [7]** where a diver has a 90 percent chance of seeing a turtle. The spur and groove formations have disappeared and are replaced with a rich variety of corals stretching from the reef crest to the drop-off.

Exactly due east of **St. George's Caye**, there are numerous patch reefs on the eastern side of the main reef. This is unusual since most patch reefs are generally found either to the west of the barrier reef or inside the atoll reefs. At St. George's Reef the patch reefs are huge, with large channels between them. Here divers will find a great variety of common reef fishes, although he is likely to be buffeted by surge in the shallow water on all but the calmest days.

At the southern end of the reef, there is a spectacular site known simply as **The Wall [8]**.

The Belize Barrier Reef, which runs parallel to the coast for 185 miles (298 km), is second in length only to Australia's Great Barrier Reef. Photo: Ned Middleton.

From the reef crest divers can follow the coral down to a depth of about 40 feet (12 m) before arriving at the top of a visually stunning vertical wall which drops straight to 150 feet (45 m) where the severity of the slope lessens.

All along this magnificent cliff is a dazzling array of life. The size of individual species grows in direct proportion to the depth. At the top of the wall, French, gray and queen angelfish are very common. Sergeant major and yellowtail damselfish dart in and out of the star, brain and staghorn corals. Foureye, spotfin and banded butterflyfish—always in pairs—swim steadily amongst the sea fans and gorgonians. Deeper, schools of grunts can be found along with medium-sized coney, graysby and snapper.

Looking seaward from the wall, divers will likely see pelagics such as jacks, tarpon and snook. Manta rays are often spotted cruising by the wall. In the distance there are always barracuda, which in spite of their fearsome appearance, are essentially benign and merely curious of divers.

Beyond a depth of about 100 feet (30 m) is big grouper country. Large tiger, red and Nassau grouper occupy almost every crevice that can accommodate them. Jewfish of massive proportions lurk here, and prime specimens of hind, coney and snapper stare back at you as if to question your right to venture into their territory.

During the months of October and November, the grouper move towards the shallow waters inside the reef and swarm in the thousands on the lee side of **Drowned Cayes [9]**. This is the mating season, and the best place for the diver to witness this marvel is to watch as the fish come up over the top of the reef at the beginning of their short migration southwest.

From January to mid-March the northwest winds prevail and these tend to stir up the water inside the reef, making it murky and blowing it down **Montego Channel** to St. George's Cut. At this time the underwater visibility can be poor, although poor visibility by Belize standards is often considered good elsewhere in the world. During the months of July through September, tarpon and snook are frequently seen in the Montego Channel and can grow to lengths of eight and four feet (2.4 and 1.2 m) respectively.

These tiny gobies are dwarfed in the mouth of a tiger grouper as they rid the fish of parasites. Photo: Keith Ibsen.

The indigo hamlet should be approached carefully since it will quickly dart away if startled. Photo: Keith Ibsen.

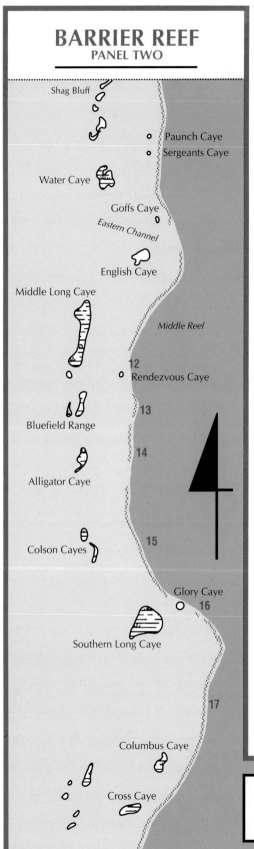

BARRIER REEF
PANEL TWO

Shag Bluff

Paunch Caye

Sergeants Caye

Water Caye

Goffs Caye

Eastern Channel

English Caye

Middle Long Caye

Middle Reef

12
Rendezvous Caye

13

Bluefield Range

14

Alligator Caye

Colson Cayes

15

Glory Caye

16

Southern Long Caye

17

Columbus Caye

Cross Caye

To the south of St. George's Cut is a stretch of reef that is one of my favorites, **Gallows Point Reef [10]**. Immediately inside the reef are shallow patch corals which are superb for snorkeling. The most common corals here are staghorn, elkhorn and brain. A rainbow variety of smaller fishes abound. The terrain on the seaward side of the reef varies considerably. To begin with, there are the shallow corals at or near the surface. These drop steadily down to 20-30 feet (6-9 m) before leveling off at a constant depth. From here it is about 200 to 400 yards (182-364 m) out to the drop-off. Along this ledge there are large patches of sand in an area called **Stingray Flats [11]** where the diver may see large stingrays digging in to lie in wait for unsuspecting prey. These patches are interspersed with coral outcrops, topped with gorgonians and sea fans. It was along this reef that I observed an oceanic white tip shark with its attendant pilotfish. Manta ray are also occasionally seen here, and there are a great many lobster. The drop-off, while not as steep as The Wall, is quite exciting, and the size and varieties of individual coral configurations are truly memorable. Gigantic and well-formed, they remain virtually the same as we move farther south along the reef and off the beaten path.

SHAG BLUFF TO CROSS CAYE
(Panel Map Two)

With so many miles of reef in Belize, it is easy to understand why much of it remains undisturbed and unexplored. It is this virgin territory that we now enter as we continue south.

Between Shag Bluff and **Goff's Caye**, there are numerous small reefs which break the surface. Very few of these have individual names, but those which have developed into small islands have become popular bar-b-que destinations for families and small groups wishing to escape for the day. Boats are essential in Belize, and the water taxis will

12. Rendezvous Caye	15. Colson Reef
13. Bluefield Reef	16. Glory Reef
14. Alligator Reef	17. Columbus Reef

Stingrays are often found on the sandy bottom between reef patches at Stingray Flats. Sometimes only their eyes protrude from the sand as they lay in wait for prey. Divers should be careful not to step on them or cause them to act defensively as the spine on their tails can inflict a painful wound. Photo: Keith Ibsen.

generally take a small group exactly where they want to go.

Paunch Caye and **Sergeants Caye** are very small, and access by boat across the shallows is difficult. However, you are virtually guaranteed the entire caye to yourself for the day and that might make the effort worthwhile. By contrast, Goff's Caye is very popular and has a limited amount of shade.

Conditions for snorkeling are excellent. The swimmer is able to get around and behind each coral promontory because they are so small. The coral extends much further at Goff's Caye which makes it the best of these cayes for snorkeling. Access to and from the water is made easier by the sandy shore, leaving just a short swim to the coral. Amongst the endless varieties of coral in these waters lives a legion of smaller sea creatures.

To the south of Goff's Caye is the main shipping channel—the entrance to **Belize City Harbor**. Diving within this clearly marked sea lane is both foolhardy and dangerous. It also serves no purpose as there is little or nothing to see.

South of the channel is **English Caye**. Slightly larger than Goff's Caye and equipped with a lighthouse, a few houses and a substantial jetty, this is another popular day-trip retreat. Unfortunately, the coral has suffered due to its proximity to the shipping channel. In addition to pollution, too much silt settling on coral eventually chokes it.

The area in the immediate vicinity of English Caye hasn't much to offer compared with the attractions farther north and south. Stingrays, however, are quite plentiful and are seen in sizes in excess of six feet (1.8 m) across.

South of English Caye are predominately spur and groove formations until you reach **Rendezvous Caye [12]**. This is a small, almost isolated island on the wrong side of the reef. It is too far from anywhere to attract regular visitors. For this reason and because it is on the seaward side of the reef, Rendezvous Caye is a rewarding place to visit.

Circumnavigating this caye underwater opens a full catalog of marine life. Those corals and fishes which thrive next to the open sea are found on the eastern side. Those that prefer a more sheltered environment are a short swim away on the west. For its size, this is one of the richest marine areas I have ever seen.

South from here the reef takes on a more familiar look. Large sections of reef break the surface and act as breakwaters.

Bluefield Reef [13] and **Alligator Reef [14]** are separated by a narrow stretch of sand. This area is home to large grouper and it is a good area to see them in great numbers coming over the top of the reef to spawn. There is little or no underwater ledge on the seaward side of the reefs. The terrain is dramatic in many places, dropping to depths in excess of 160 feet (50 m). There are no disappointing dives along this entire stretch. The sea is teeming with fishes, and, as before: the deeper the dive, the bigger the fishes. The corals seem to clamber over one another in competition for attention.

Caution. When swimming along the reef with the bottom of this spectacular wall a blur in the distance below, divers must keep a careful eye on depth. There are many places in Belize where it is easy to stray over the planned limit, and this is one of them. Free-falling through the water in slow motion, all manner of creatures dart before your eyes. There are so many distractions to take the mind away from dive safety.

Colson Reef [15] is known for its Spanish mackerel and king mackerel which apparently like to feed around **Colson Caye**. These predatory fish grow very large, and the fortunate diver may see them swimming over the reef towards their favorite feeding grounds. The best visibility is found near the gaps at the northern and southern ends of the reef. There is a wide stretch of water behind the reef which is virtually free of obstructions. This provides a safe passage for small boats, and is continually used by divers and fishermen. This waterway was dubbed **The Yellow Brick Road** a few years ago by Ray Bowers and the name has stuck.

In contrast to this safe passage, on top of Colson Reef are two wrecks. Unfortunately, they are too high out of the water to be of use to divers.

A delightful underwater ledge runs the length of **Glory Caye** at a depth of 30-40 feet (9-12 m) and forms part of **Glory Reef [16]**. Here is an underwater garden ringed with luxuriant coral and bursting with marine life, with some of the best underwater visibility to be found anywhere. To the south of this reef is a large sandy patch which slopes right down to the reef wall.

To the south is **Columbus Reef [17]** which breaks the surface continuously for almost 14 miles (23 km). This reef is out of the protection of the offshore Turneffe Islands. Lemon shark, manta ray, small groups of large spotted eagle ray and the occasional oceanic white tip shark make diving this reef a memorable experience. The drop-off starts between 40 and 70 feet (12-21 m) and continues down to abysmal depths. This vital reef is a wellspring of psychedelic colors and animated marine life.

From the predominance of staghorn coral near the surface, the reef falls away vertically to depths in excess of 200 feet (61 m), but the main attractions are in shallow water. There are gullies which turn into tunnels where divers can swim beneath a roof of living coral. To each side there are offshoots creating a maze in which only the largest lobsters are found. Nurse sharks are frequently found resting on the many ledges.

At some time during every dive, one should pause and reflect on the entire scene. Here, along Columbus Reef, the diver will be aware of this extensive formation as a single living entity, and the harmony of natural systems which served to create it.

TOBACCO CAYE TO QUEEN CAYE
(Panel Map Three)

Towards the southern end of Columbus Reef, the underwater ledge reappears and is a feature of the remainder of the barrier reef. **Tobacco Caye** is situated right at the southern tip of Columbus Reef. Inside the reef, between this caye and **Tobacco Range**, is one of the most curious dive sites I have ever encountered. Known as the **Shark Pit [18]**, but often referred to as **Hell's Hole**, this aperture in the sand drops straight down to 110 feet (33 m) and opens into a huge underground cavern. The cavern is always full of sharks and is an exciting opportunity for underwater photographers. This dive is only for advanced divers.

At **Tobacco Cut [19]** there exists a splendid array of shallow-water corals in an arc formation which points towards the mainland. Almost all the common varieties are found here with brain coral predominant, followed by superb arrangements of staghorn and elkhorn. Tarpon and other large fishes are regularly seen here.

Tobacco Reef [20] is an area of great scientific interest and has been the subject of several surveys. These are ongoing projects, and detailed information is being collected on the effects of pollution and uncontrolled exploitation. Coral reefs are one of the most complex and diverse environments to be found anywhere on earth and have been in existence for over 450 million years. But, like the rain forests of Central and South America, they have become increasingly threatened by man.

Tobacco Reef was selected for these studies for a number of reasons. Tobacco Caye and **Water Caye** are small, inhabited islands offering a suitable expedition base. With the mangroves west of the reef, they make prime

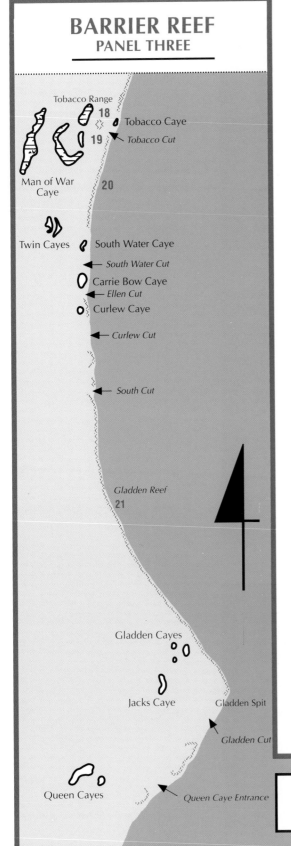

BARRIER REEF
PANEL THREE

Tobacco Range

18 Tobacco Caye

19 *Tobacco Cut*

Man of War Caye

20

Twin Cayes

South Water Caye

South Water Cut

Carrie Bow Caye

Ellen Cut

Curlew Caye

Curlew Cut

South Cut

Gladden Reef

21

Gladden Cayes

Jacks Caye

Gladden Spit

Gladden Cut

Queen Cayes

Queen Caye Entrance

examples of the mangrove-foreshore-reef ecosystem which is sustained along much of the Belize Barrier Reef. Tobacco Reef can also produce an example of almost every species of flora and fauna known to these latitudes.

Tobacco Reef consists of well-formed spur and groove patterns. Along the entire reef, the spurs are laced with exciting holes, tunnels and swim-throughs. This is one of the finest areas anywhere for seeing the spotted eagle ray. One diving instructor claims to have seen a minimum of 25 of these magnificent fish on every dive. I thought I had seen large eagles before, but these are huge and possibly the largest specimens that exist. Turtles also frequent Tobacco Reef, and in May this is a good place to look for the whale shark.

It is said that it was the manatee which gave rise to the legend of the mermaid. If this is true, then those sailors were certainly out of sight of women for a very long time. The manatee, sometimes called the sea cow or dugong (technically a different genus of the same order), does not generally inhabit those areas which are of interest to divers. Instead it prefers the murky, brackish waters of the estuary, occasionally venturing out as far as the mangroves. Manatees have been observed off Goff's Caye and, with some frequency, immediately west of Tobacco Reef amongst **Tobacco Shallows** and **Man of War Caye**. The manatee is totally harmless and will allow the diver to approach and even to pet their young. Of course, it should always be remembered that this mammal is an endangered species.

The area between Water Caye and **South Cut** is known to have deceived many Spanish galleons with what appears to be a large gap between two reefs, where there is actually little safe passage. Looking for shelter during a storm, or seeking water (there are fresh-water wells on most cayes), many ships came to grief on the shallow sand bottom and the many small outcrops of patch coral. As yet, most of these wrecks remain hidden under the sand and await the attention of marine

| 18. Shark Pit | 20. Tobacco Reef |
| 19. Tobacco Cut | 21. Gladden Reef |

The delicate red-banded coral shrimp is found everywhere on the reef. Check carefully under ledges and in small crevices for a glimpse of these tiny creatures. Photo: Ned Middleton.

A blenny peers out from its home in the ridges of a brain coral. Photo: Keith Ibsen.

The colors of the lantern bass often blend with the reef, making it more difficult to spot. Photo: Keith Ibsen.

BARRIER REEF
PANEL FOUR

Round Caye

Pompion Caye

Ranguana Caye

North Spot

Tom Owen's Cayes

Seal Caye

Frank's Caye

Nicholas Caye

Hunting Caye   22

Lime Caye

Ragged Caye

22. Hunting Caye

archaeologists. This same area, however, is ideal for large stingrays and spotted eagle rays. The patch reefs are alive with the delicate colors of damselfishes, butterflyfishes and wrasse, which find refuge in the coral crevices when divers approach.

Gladden Reef [21] is the last major reef in the system. It is almost 15 miles (24 km) of unbroken radiance, resplendent in coral, fishes and minute organisms of every variety. This is one of the reefs in Belize where I have seen the bull shark. The excitement is electrifying as these creatures encircle the diving group twice—the second pass always a little closer than the first—then decide that there's nothing there to interest them after all.

Never more than half a mile wide (.8 km), the underwater ledge which runs the length of Gladden Reef varies from 30 to 40 feet (9-12 m) deep near the reef and 60 to 80 feet (18-24 m) at the very edge. Outcrops of coral interspersed with small patches of sand are crested with gorgonians and sea fans in a kaleidoscopic array of colors, gently wafting with any hint of surface action. Pufferfish, scrawled filefish, cowfish, trunkfish and queen triggerfish are in great abundance here.

ROUND CAYE TO LIME CAYE
(Panel Map Four)

From **Gladden Cut** all the way down to **Hunting Caye**, there are large areas of sand punctuated with patch reefs which appear to arise out of nowhere. These smaller reefs do not have enough unique attractions and are too remote to lure many divers. In addition, the patch reefs are particularly dangerous for larger diving vessels to navigate. The large expanse of sand does, however, like the area above South Cut, hide some of the world's long forgotten shipwrecks, and someday will undoubtedly yield finds of great interest.

Hunting Caye [22] is a small, crescent-shaped island less than a half mile (.8 km) long. The main beach is made of the finest crushed coral. The surrounding waters are deceptive: the reef runs along the eastern side of the caye and there are few safe passages. Most boats approach from the western side and tie up at the main jetty, but one has to know the waters well.

The caye is occupied by a small contingent of police and local defense forces. There is an important lighthouse which marks the southern

An old broken-up shipwreck south of Hunting Caye provides refuge for thousands of fishes that congregate there. Photo: Ned Middleton.

One of the more vibrantly-colored fishes of the reef is the fairy basslet. They are very shy and difficult to approach. Photo: Keith Ibsen.

extremity of the barrier reef. The lightkeeper and the caretaker live on the island with their families and provide useful information for visiting divers. On weekends, up to 200 people arrive, mainly from Guatemala and Honduras, for a day trip to the beach. I would recommend visiting during the week.

South of Hunting Caye, inside the reef, is a large area of sand and sea grass. Conch, turtle, and large rays are common. The area is also shallow and clear. Immmediately to the east, right on the reef itself, is an old wreck where fish congregate by the thousands. The wreck is well broken up and is not even marked on the chart. The rudder and two boilers are still easily identifiable, as is part of the superstructure and an old cast iron propellor. According to the locals, the boat was either a trawler or a tug that struck the reef in the 1940's. Fifty years of tropical storms and

An encounter with a whale shark is certainly the highlight of any dive trip. Here along the southern end of the Barrier Reef these large plankton-eating pelagics are often seen feeding in the shallow waters. Photo: Keith Ibsen.

continual wave action have reduced the wreck to little more than a small extension of the reef.

A short distance farther north is a very large admiralty-pattern anchor in 40 feet (12 m) of water. The local story is that some years ago a Guatemalan gunboat anchored here and refused to move when requested to do so. Eventually the boat was buzzed by the Royal Air Force and the crew moved so quickly that they saved time by jettisoning the anchor.

Cannon have been found to the north of Hunting Caye. Two were recently found just to the north of **Nicholas Caye**. This is another area for a concentrated search for old wrecks.

To the south, off **Lime Caye**, the locals fish for sharks and regularly catch bull sharks among others. They use a system of two weighted buoys tied together with a long line from which hang the baited hooks. The buoys have blue flags and for obvious reasons, it is a good idea for divers to avoid the area.

For me the southern end of the Belize Barrier Reef is exciting because of the possibility of encountering one of the world's most magnificent creatures—the whale shark. Passing the end of the reef, these mighty leviathans appear to find feeding in the shallow water much to their liking.

CHAPTER **VI** TURNEFFE ISLANDS

Reef Roundup

The Turneffe Islands make up the largest of the three offshore atoll reefs in Belize and also are the most accessible from the mainland. Unlike the other two—Glovers and Lighthouse—there are over 200 cayes within the reef which are covered with mangroves. These have created land, lagoons, creeks and expansive flats. There are a few routes through from one side to the other, but these should only be attempted by those who know the waters well.

The entire eastern shoreline is protected by a continuous vertical reef approximately 35 miles (56 km) long. From the crest of this reef, a narrow ledge falls away over a distance of about 100 yards (91 m) until it reaches an average depth of between 55 and 65 feet (17-18 m) where the drop-off begins. Along this ledge are a number of spur and groove formations which are host to a myriad of reef fishes.

At a depth of approximately 150 feet (45 m) is a horizontal ridge with another at 250 feet (76 m). These ridges extend throughout the length of the reef and are an example of wave erosion when water levels were much lower than today.

There are few navigable entrances through the reef. In the southeast there is **North Cut**, some 400 yards (121 m) south of **Cocoa Tree Caye**. A little further south is **South Cut** just 150 yards (45 m) from **Big Caye Bokel**. The depth of both channels is only 8 feet (2.4 m) so their use is limited to small craft. They both provide access into the **South Lagoon** where a dive resort is situated on **Caye Bokel**.

On the southwest corner of the atoll there are entrances at **Pirates Creek** just above Big Caye Bokel, and **Blue Creek**, two miles (3.2 km) further to the north. Both entrances are only 5 feet (1.5 m) deep at the mouth although they do deepen to 8 and 13 feet (2.4 and 4 m)

respectively. Any craft entering through these channels must exercise extreme caution. The mangroves create murky water inside the atoll and this obscures underwater obstacles.

Further north there is **Rendezvous Cut** on the west coast and **Eastern Cut** on the opposite side of the atoll. These entrances are much larger and are used by the diving trade from San Pedro. En route to Lighthouse Reef, the dive boats arrive at the Turneffe Islands about mid-morning and usually dive at a site not far from Rendezvous Cut. Afterwards the boats enter through the cut and anchor long enough to allow the passengers a light lunch before proceeding through Eastern Cut and across to Lighthouse Reef.

Ecologically this is a fascinating atoll reef. Unlike west of the barrier reef, the mangroves are completely surrounded by the sea. For this reason the wind, tides and gentle currents all combine to distribute the nutrients propagated in the mangroves around the reef. This is part of a cycle that is continually, if unknowingly, witnessed by the divers who visit the reef.

On the east coast in particular, there are massive concentrations of fishes which come in close to the reef to feed. Here are the largest shoals of fishes I have ever seen. Hovering between 50 and 80 feet (15-24 m) are shoals of horse-eye jack, crevalle jack, black snapper, cubera snapper, mutton snapper and permit.

Angelfishes, such as this intermediate French angelfish, are amongst the most curious of reef fishes. The adults are usually seen as mated pairs swimming in unison around the reef. Photo: Keith Ibsen.

There are literally thousands of fish in a single shoal with more than one shoal often in sight. Individual fish sizes range from 5 to 30 pounds (2-4 kg), but the size of all fish in any single shoal is always uniform, as they were spawned together and have grown together. The diver will frequently encounter this in shallow water where the fish will be 2 or 3 inches (5 or 8 cm) long, but as the fish grow they tend to disperse as they need more individual space to feed. Here, the concentration of nutrients and the resultant populations of smaller fish is so great as to sustain shoals of larger fish which feed on them. These, in turn, attract the pelagics, and

lemon, Caribbean reef, blacktip and the occasional solitary hammerhead shark can be seen here.

Manta rays also put in an appearance, and green and hawksbill turtles are usually seen. Bottlenose and spotted dolphin often fish these waters. A family of six to eight bottlenose dolphins live in **South Lagoon** and regularly swim to within a few feet of the shore. A real treat in this area is the abundance of spotted eagle rays. One diver counted no fewer than 31 of these splendid creatures in a single dive.

The drop-off on the eastern side of the reef begins at 80 feet (24 m). Venturing deeper,

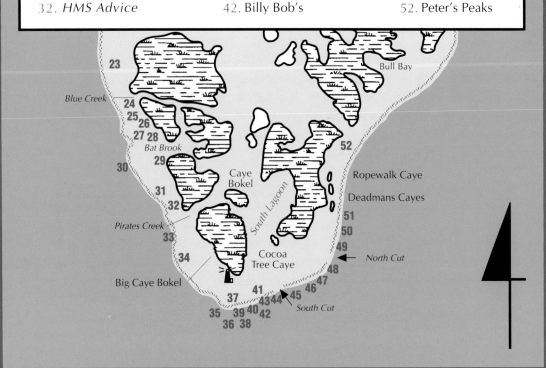

SOUTHERN TURNEFFE ISLANDS

23. The Aquarium	33. West Point Wall	43. Black Beauty
24. Triple Anchors	34. Cabbage Patch	44. Majestic Point
25. Hollywood	35. The Elbow	45. T's Trail
26. Susie's Shallows	36. The Corral	46. Cut Throat
27. Permit Paradise	37. Myrtle's Turtles	47. Front Porch
28. *Sayonara*	38. Lefty's Ledge	48. Gail's Point
29. Bat Brook Shallows	39. Joyce's Jump	49. The Secret Spot
30. Jill's Thrill	40. Gorgonian Bluff	50. Fabian's Roost
31. Randolph's Rocks	41. Billy Bob's Shallows	51. Birthday Reef
32. *HMS Advice*	42. Billy Bob's	52. Peter's Peaks

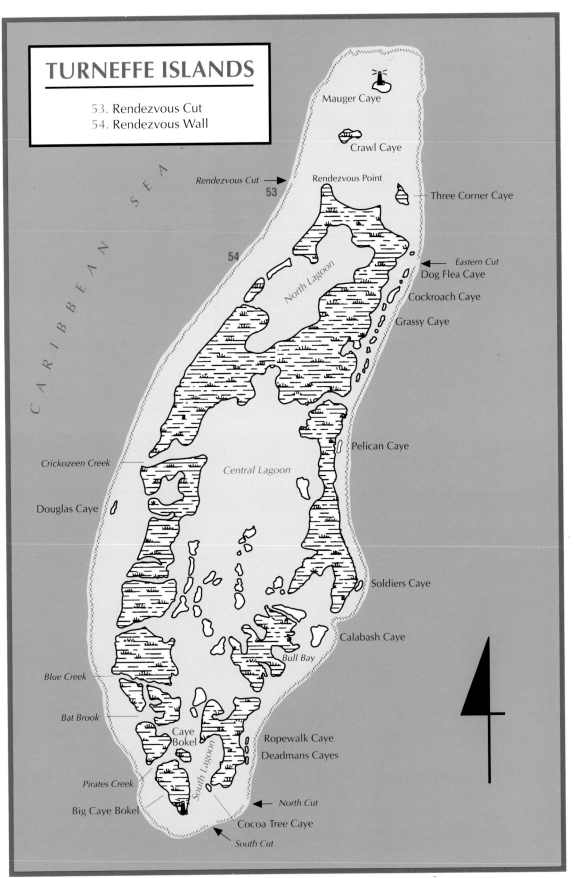

TURNEFFE ISLANDS

Mauger Caye

Crawl Caye

Rendezvous Cut → **53** Rendezvous Point

Three Corner Caye

54

North Lagoon

← *Eastern Cut*
Dog Flea Caye

Cockroach Caye

Grassy Caye

Pelican Caye

Crickozeen Creek

Central Lagoon

Douglas Caye

C A R I B B E A N   S E A

Soldiers Caye

Calabash Caye

Bull Bay

Blue Creek

Bat Brook

Caye Bokel

Ropewalk Caye

Deadmans Cayes

Pirates Creek

Big Caye Bokel

South Lagoon

← *North Cut*

Cocoa Tree Caye

South Cut

53

Huge shoals of fish come in close to the reef to feed along the eastern side of the Turneffe Islands. Photo: Ned Middleton.

divers will encounter some truly formidable scenery. Occasionally a large shoal will be silhouetted against the sun above the diver. Apart from the grouper and jewfish always associated with deeper waters, there are other surprises here. Tuna, especially skip jack tuna, and Spanish and king mackerel are common. Wahoo and cero are less common but still regularly sighted. On rare occasions divers have come face to face with an Atlantic blue marlin or a sailfish.

Throughout the remainder of the western coastline there are many creeks and cuts between the mangrove cayes within the atoll. The prevailing easterly winds have the effect of blowing sand and silt westwards and this has a detrimental effect on the reef. Coral that is constantly subjected to silt and other sediment eventually chokes and dies. This is all too obvious when comparisons are made between the different reef structures and their condition on either side of the atoll.

On the west, spur and groove formations dominate the underwater scenery with too many wide grooves of sand and few spurs of coral. There are one or two exceptions, but nobody searches for diving which is good to mediocre when excellent diving is found elsewhere on the atoll. This complete change of underwater terrain is a feature of this atoll reef alone and is largely due to the great number of mangroves which are absent on the other two atoll reefs.

All is not doom and gloom, however. Large spotted eagle rays patrol the coast, and where there is a coral spur it is always surrounded by a plentiful supply of common reef tropicals. Lobster also flourish because the area is not very popular with fishermen.

The northern tip of the atoll is buffeted constantly by the long Caribbean swells and is unsuitable for diving most of the time. The reef crest reappears and north of this the underwater ledge is very wide. Nurse sharks are likely to be encountered during the dive, and for once divers will see them swimming and not resting on a ledge. The best bet for the photographer is to keep absolutely still and wait for the shark to swim towards him. This requires a degree of patience and silence by

Mangroves with their masses of roots are found on many of Belize's cayes and are especially prolific on the Turneffe Islands. Nutrients propagated in the mangroves are responsible for the dense shoals of fish found on the eastern side of Turneffe. Photo: Ned Middleton.

everyone in the group, but is often rewarded.

Those divers who know the Turneffe Islands intimately will swear that the diving is far superior to anywhere else. Certainly the effects of the mangroves on the fish population make this atoll particularly interesting, but as to which is the best diving I really cannot say. The barrier reef and each of the three atolls all have their own unique features.

Squid are more readily seen during a night dive. Photo: Keith Ibsen.

Specific Dive Sites

Listed below are a variety of dive sites around the southern end of the atoll reef and two on the western side. The shallower sites are all very good for night diving although some are better than others. Difficulty of access by boat at night does, however, preclude night diving at some very good sites.

23. THE AQUARIUM

This shallow setting is reminiscent of a household aquarium. It is very clean and tidy, with a variety of small corals and a profusion of small reef fishes including almost every variety of grunt. The maximum depth is 12 feet (3.6 m), so it is an ideal site for the last dive of the day. It's a good spot for underwater photography.

24. TRIPLE ANCHORS

This site is named for three very large anchors lying at a depth of 45 feet (14 m) dating from the mid- to late 1700's. No wreck has ever been found here, so most likely they were slipped when the anchorage became dangerous during a storm. The site is buoyed.

25. HOLLYWOOD

Big coral heads and outcrops start at a depth of 35 feet (11 m) and stretch down to 60 feet (18 m). These coral formations are large and wide with mountainous star coral being the most dominant variety. Numerous tunnels, arches, nooks and swim-throughs make this a fascinating dive site.

26. SUSIE'S SHALLOWS

Susie's is another shallow dive ideal for rounding off the day. The maximum depth is only 15 feet (5 m) and the coral heads rise up to within a few feet of the surface. All the reef fishes can be found here. It is an especially good place to photograph the radiant rock beauty.

27. PERMIT PARADISE

The permit, a large member of the pompano family much prized by the serious game fisherman, is a regular visitor to this area. Here a horseshoe-shaped curve cuts into the coral on the very edge of the reef. Coral types and patterns are very similar to the Hollywood site. The depth here is 60 feet (18 m).

28. *SAYONARA*

The *Sayonara* was the transport boat for the Turneffe Island Lodge. It was taken out of service and sunk as a dive site in 1985. The wreckage lies in 40 to 45 feet (12-14 m) and is rapidly deteriorating. The wreck has become the hangout for a number of fishes which are used to being fed by divers. The site is buoyed.

29. BAT BROOK SHALLOWS

Inside the reef on this southwest corner of the atoll is a wide area between the cayes and the reef. This entire corner, with its shallow diving conditions of only 15 feet (5 m), is ideal for repetitive dives. This site is very similar to Susie's Shallows although the fish life is different, with French and gray angelfish in the "young adult" stage of their development being particularly common.

A vase sponge and orange encrusting sponge are overshadowed by a giant barrel sponge on the lip of the drop-off. Photo: Keith Ibsen.

30. JILL'S THRILL

Situated right on the edge of the wall is Jill's Thrill, one of only two wall dives off the southwest side of the atoll. Right along this corner of the reef the coral drops sharply to 60 feet (18 m). The reef then slopes gradually over a distance of 100 yards (91 m) down to a depth of 110 feet (33 m) where we find this site. On the edge of the reef wall the coral reaches up again to within 60 to 65 feet (18-20 m) of the surface before dropping down. Schooling cero, Spanish mackerel and small groups of spotted eagle rays are regularly seen here.

31. RANDOLPH'S ROCKS

At an average depth of about 60 feet (18 m) are a series of scattered coral heads and boulders resting on a flat surface. Giant brain corals are especially prevalent as are deep water gorgonians which provide attractive cover for all kinds of smaller reef fishes and crustaceans.

32. *HMS ADVICE*

Located just outside Pirate's Creek in 16 feet (5 m) of water are the remains of a British naval cutter which was wrecked on June 1, 1793. With a length of 56 feet (17 m) and a beam of 21 feet (6 m), the vessel carried ten 3-pounder guns. It is likely that the guns were salvaged long ago because of the shallow water, although the site is worth a search with an underwater metal detector. After almost 200 years, little is left of the actual ship except for three anchors and some mast rings. Observant divers are occasionally rewarded with buttons, brass spikes and broken bottles, so the area is worth a good dig around.

33. WEST POINT WALL

This is the second of the wall dives on the southwest corner of the atoll. Two coral ridges, each 35 to 40 feet (11-12 m) long, protrude horizontally from the vertical reef wall. They are 65 feet (20 m) apart and both ridges can be visited during a single dive. Several large fish shoals, as well as some pelagics, are seen here, but they are not as plentiful as on the eastern coast. Nevertheless, the coral is crowned with a good display of gorgonians and the dive site is memorable for the striking coral compositions which are very different from elsewhere.

34. CABBAGE PATCH

Between the lighthouse and the reef is a pristine area of staghorn, elkhorn, brain and lettuce leaf corals. These varieties are found all around the southern end of the atoll, but the beauty of this particular spot is quite unbelievable. It is an excellent spot for divers who wish to photograph species of coral. Here, like elsewhere in the shallower waters, are all the common reef fishes. Angelfishes, butterflyfishes, squirrelfishes, parrotfishes, grunts, damselfishes and even queen triggerfish are all present in good numbers along with several species of moray eel. Large tarpon are often seen between here and *HMS Advice*.

35. THE ELBOW
36. THE CORRAL

These two sites are close together, but are dived separately by the local dive trade. While currents are hardly experienced in Belize, these are both drift dives situated at the southern tip of the atoll reef. The currents provide a natural concentration of food which accounts for the greater number of fish shoals and pelagic life. The Corral has a constant depth of 90 feet (27 m) and can be undertaken by most divers. The Elbow is at the very southern tip and is for the advanced diver only. The average depth at the beginning of the Elbow site is 90 feet (27 m) and usually ends at 120 to 140 feet (36-42 m). Here are some of the largest gorgonians to be found anywhere. Swaying gently with the current, they create a

Large gorgonians are one of the many attractions that make a drift dive at The Elbow a memorable experience. Photo: Keith Ibsen.

Tube sponges can be found throughout Belize's reef system. They often have tiny shrimp inside the tube. Photo: Ned Middleton.

marvelous backdrop to the fish life encountered as the diver drifts gently past.

37. MYRTLE'S TURTLES

At one specific spot on the southern point, a large green turtle called Myrtle has appeared every spring for the past 12 years. Myrtle is totally unafraid of divers and even allows herself to be touched. Myrtle's presence also attracts other turtles.

38. LEFTY'S LEDGE

39. JOYCE'S JUMP

40. GORGONIAN BLUFF

These are three separate sites situated close together with similar features. At the edge of the reef wall, there is an awesome hand-shaped coral promontory with three "fingers" outstretched, each with a different name. At the tips, these fingers are 50 to 60 feet (15-18 m) apart and approximately 60 feet (18 m) deep. The last of the fingers, Gorgonian Bluff, is well known for its magnificent display of deep water gorgonians. Blacktip sharks are regularly seen at all three sites.

41. BILLY BOB'S SHALLOWS

Along the southeast corner of Big Caye Bokel in shallow water averaging 25 feet (8 m), are scattered coral heads with splendid structures of elkhorn and staghorn, as well as other types of coral. This is a pristine area and one of the few which attracts reef squid and octopus.

42. BILLY BOB'S

43. BLACK BEAUTY

44. MAJESTIC POINT

These three sites offer some delightful spur and groove formations which have created canyons, tunnels and exciting swim-throughs. As the canyons narrow, the corals combine to create a sheer cliff between the depths of 70 and 150 feet (21-45 m). Black Beauty was

named after a magnificent growth of black coral which was over 10 feet (3 m) high and 8 feet (2m) across. It is deplorable that in a single day in 1989, one man removed it all. Majestic Point is just that—a majestic collection of corals in a stunning formation.

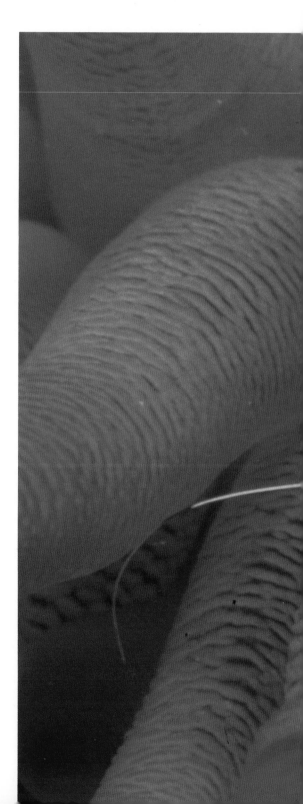

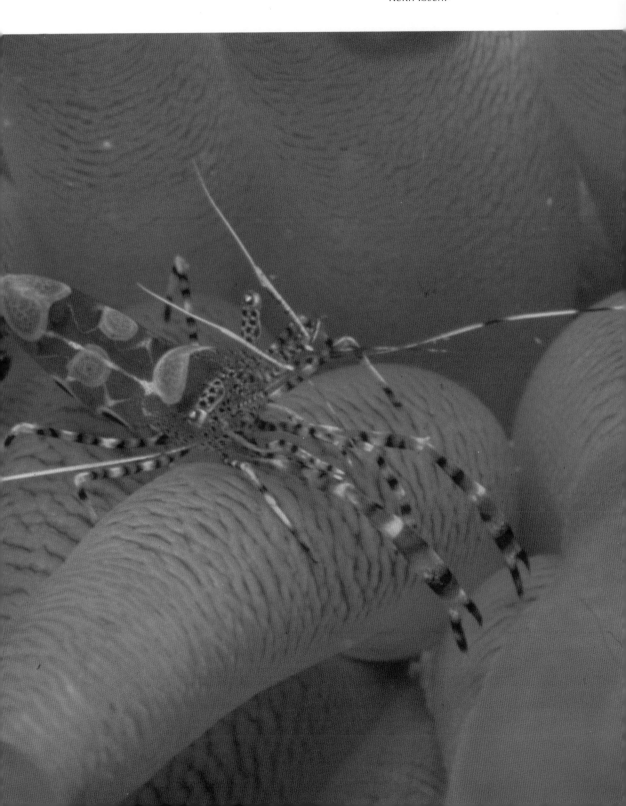

By paying close attention to detail, divers can be rewarded with some of Belize's most delicate underwater creatures such as this spotted cleaner shrimp perched within the tentacles of a pink-tipped anemone. Photo: Keith Ibsen.

Inspect the walls carefully for small creatures when swimming slowly through Cut Throat, a narrow groove cutting through the coral. Photo: Ned Middleton.

The main feature of the dive sites known as The Secret Spot, Fabian's Roost and Birthday Reef is the wall. This magnificent precipice is a fine example of Belize underwater at its best. Photo: Joe Miller.

45. T'S TRAIL

46. CUT THROAT

47. FRONT PORCH

48. GAIL'S POINT

Although located very close together, these are separate dive sites. Lots of shallow grooves cut through the coral at a depth of 45 to 60 feet (14-18 m) at all these sites. Over the reef wall are undercuts which create massive overhangs. There are also a number of ledges and a rarely equaled profusion of tube and barrel sponges.

It was here that 31 spotted eagle rays were seen during a single dive. Gail's Point is the southeast corner of the reef, and divers will notice a change in the coral structures when heading north. This is the beginning of the dramatic vertical wall which continues along the eastern reef line.

49. THE SECRET SPOT

50. FABIAN'S ROOST

51. BIRTHDAY REEF

The main feature of these three sites is the vertical reef wall. From the reef crest, the underwater terrain gradually falls away over a distance of about 100 yards (91 m) to a depth of 60 feet (18 m). Here begins the drop-off—an amazing precipice which is an example of Belizean underwater beauty at its best. Even the novice diver can savor this wall as it begins in relatively shallow water. Mountainous star, brain (including the giant brain coral) and finger corals are intermixed with large tube and barrel sponges. This is the beginning of big fish country, and by that I mean big fish in big numbers as they shoal lazily just above the drop-off. To the east is the open water of the Caribbean so pelagics are often seen, including the rare oceanic whitetip shark.

52. PETER'S PEAKS

The bottom here slopes away to a depth of about 35 feet (11 m). At this point the diver is confronted by an imposing wall of living coral. To get to the other side, you can either swim up to about 15 feet (5 m) and cross over the top of the wall, or you can find one of the many tunnels in the coral. Entering at 35 feet (11 m), you invariably come out the other side closer to 60 feet (18 m). This is very exciting diving.

53. RENDEZVOUS CUT

It is here, close to Rendezvous Cut on the western side of the atoll, that the diving trade from San Pedro give their customers a first dive when on a two-day visit to Lighthouse Reef. There is no reef crest so the boats anchor above the underwater ledge and have a large expanse to choose from.

At 40 to 50 feet (12-15 m) the seabed consists of outcrops of the most common corals. Generally rising only a few feet (1 m) above the sand, there are occasionally much larger coral heads, usually giant brain, although very large branches of elkhorn are

also seen. In amongst the various nooks and crannies are all the popular reef fishes the diver has come to expect: angelfishes—especially the decorative rock beauty—butterflyfishes, trunkfishes and even small shoals of boxfishes. Green moray eels are also quite common.

For a number of people, this is the first taste of Belize underwater. Listening to them after the dive, the comments are indeed favorable and they are generally glad to have made the journey and experienced such good diving. But soon the memory of this particular dive will have become rather vague as they begin to discover what Belize really has to offer.

54. RENDEZVOUS WALL

One of the most curious dive sites I have ever encountered is just to the south of Rendezvous Cut and is known as Rendezvous Wall. The reef wall commences at a depth of 35 feet (11 m), below which is a well-formed overhang. At a depth of 135 feet (41 m), in the center of this overhang, is a hole. To be exact, it is a small tunnel (too small for the diver to enter) formed by rainfall cutting through the limestone substrata when the sea levels were much lower than today. This tunnel connects right through to one of the lagoons inside the atoll and has become a fresh water outflow from that lagoon. Both the freshwater and the silt kill the coral and have not only created the overhang but have also caused the white appearance of the surrounding corals, which are known as the "icebergs."

CHAPTER **VII**   GLOVER'S REEF

REEF ROUNDUP

Glover's Reef is the most southerly of Belize's three atoll reefs and is easily the most overlooked. Yet if this reef were transported to any other Caribbean country, it would immediately become a major diving destination. It is because Belize has so much to offer that this particular atoll is often neglected.

Glover's Reef has 40 miles (65 km) of reef "coastline" as well as numerous small patch reefs inside the perimeter. These are not deep enough for diving, but do provide excellent snorkeling. The outer edge of the reef is surrounded by a ledge which is never less than 800 yards (727 m) wide and is up to 2 miles (3 km) wide at both the northeast and southwest corners.

There are four passages through the reef: **South Channel** in the south, **North Channel** in the northeast, **West Cut** in the west and **Long Caye Cut** in the east. West Cut is often used by small fishing and diving craft where the skippers know the waters and reef intimately. Those who don't should not attempt this passage. There are seven cayes in this atoll, six of which are scattered along the eastern side towards the south. **North Caye** is located in the north.

Coral growth is always far more intense in the shallower water. Even though any reef wall is dramatic to look at, vibrant coral growth at the surface eventually pales as the diver ventures deeper. Glover's Reef is almost an exception to the rule. Massive corals, for which the entire atoll is famous, reach down as far as 110 feet (33 m). There is plenty of black coral and creative arrangements of lettuce coral in amongst the more common varieties.

Anyone wishing to photograph Caribbean marine life should begin around this splendid atoll. The sheer variety is extraordinary. Dolphin, spotted eagle rays and a variety of turtles are seen all year round. The best months for seeing whale sharks are April to June, and the biggest grouper and jewfish are sighted in January.

The eastern side of the atoll which comprises a continuous wall is the most dramatic. Here the reef faces the Caribbean Sea and there are sand chutes, tunnels and a variety of structures which combine to make this intriguing diving. The underwater terrain eventually falls away almost vertically to 2,600 feet (788 m).

Northern Dip, as the north coast is called, suffers from a surfeit of long, rolling Caribbean swells on all but the calmest of days. This makes diving difficult and reduces underwater visibility. However, when conditions permit the diving is well worth the visit. The ledge begins at 40 to 50 feet (12-15 m) immediately below the reef crest, and over a distance of about 800 yards (727 m) gradually drops to a depth of about 120 feet (36 m). Long strips of coral separated by sand strips of varying widths give the ledge the appearance of a well-cultivated field.

The largest specimens of stingray are to be found half-buried in the sand with their large eyes protruding as they watch and await their prey. Small shoals of goatfishes, busily sifting the sand, are never far away.

A juvenile threespot damselfish takes refuge amongst columns of pillar coral. Photo: Keith Ibsen.

Christmas tree worms live in tubes and spread their plumes to catch plankton and small food particles. If their light-sensitive eyes detect the slightest shadow, they will rapidly retract. Photo: Keith Ibsen.

On the northeast side, the reef approaches the surface and the turbulence can limit visibility. Staghorn, elkhorn and countless other corals create yet another perfect habitat for all the common reef tropicals: damselfishes, butterflyfishes, tang, surgeonfishes and grunts. There are many juveniles here as well, and quite often they bear absolutely no resemblance to the adult.

The ledge, which runs along the length of the reef, slopes gently down to the drop-off some distance away. Starting at about 35 feet (11 m) and down to 80 to 100 feet (24-30 m) where the drop-off begins, divers can enjoy endless varieties of flora and fauna. Along the wall itself, splendid examples of barrel and tube sponges jut out from the vertical coral wall. While they are not as numerous as on the southeast corner of Turneffe, each of these sponges is very large. Shoals of creole wrasse,

propelled by pectoral fins only, will surround divers. All along this wall there are the larger species, such as jewfish and grouper, as well as frequent sightings of oceanic whitetip sharks and manta rays.

The long, unbroken reef on the western side of the atoll is quite different. Above the reef wall the slopes are gentler with many more turtles to be found. The diving is varied and interesting and, being on the lee shore, far more popular. Large spurs of coral, with grooves of differing widths, stand above a drop-off which is not as steep as on the eastern side, and begins to level off at 140 to 160 feet (42-50 m). In places, the coral rises up to within 10 feet (3 m) of the surface. Whether a diver chooses a route up and over the coral, or through one of the many tunnels and gaps, he will be surrounded by magnificent coral in a state of exceptionally good health.

GLOVERS REEF

CARIBBEAN SEA

Northwest Elbow 68

SS Venture 7
Northern Dip

67
Grouper Point

SS Alps

65
North Caye

66
North Channel

Steel Trawler

OVER 700 SHALLOW PATCH REEFS

69

SS Hilda G

West Cut

70

Lamont Caye
Northeast Caye 63 64 ← Long Caye Cut
Long Caye
Long Reef
62

71 Middle Caye

61

72
Manta Reef
Lagoon 60 Southwest Cayes
73 55 59
74 56 57 58
South Channel

Although two wrecks are marked on Admiralty Chart 1797, there is little to be found at either site. There are three other sites on the northeast corner of the atoll. However, the sea at this point is generally turbulent, making the surface conditions and the underwater visibility unpredictable. I have been unable to discover any information about these wrecks, but they are generally considered to be about 200 years old. Divers are still finding artifacts at each site.

A number of vessels are known to have come to grief on Glover's Reef. Off the north coast, the **Venture 7** was wrecked in 1973. Off Grouper Point, the **Alps** perished in 1917, while further south a steel trawler ended her sailing days near North Channel. In 1971 the **Hilda G** was lost off the east coast and disappeared over the drop-off into water far too deep for scuba diving.

SPECIFIC DIVE SITES

There are so many good dive sites that it was difficult to limit my selection. I have tried to include representative sites from around the atoll reef.

55. CORAL CUT

This site is at the southern tip of the atoll in the middle of the South Channel, one of only four gaps through the entire reef. The seabed here is covered with an array of staghorn, elkhorn, brain, massive leaf, ribbon and other corals. As is always the case in shallower water, it is the smaller fish which dominate the scenery against this backdrop of coral crowned with gently swaying gorgonians and sea fans of wildly contrasting colors. With a depth of only 25-30 feet (8-10 m), it is ideal for the last dive of the day and is a dive to remember for its variety.

56. LINCOLN TUNNEL

Divers can be forgiven for thinking Lincoln Tunnel, situated just below Manta Point, is nothing more than a barren expanse of sand. This is one of the few areas in Belize where a colony of garden eels can be found. Looking like sparse vegetation, the eels disappear into

their holes in the sand when divers approach. Moving seaward to the reef, divers are confronted with a coral promontory in which there is a single tunnel where a huge jewfish usually resides.

57. GORGONIA GALLERY

Close by and immediately south of Southwest Caye is a wall literally covered with a marvelous display of gorgonians of every color imaginable. From the palest green to the deepest purple, this is the thickest concentration I have ever seen, and their sychronized swaying in the ocean currents is mesmerizing.

58. OCTOPUS ALLEY

This site is just east of Southwest Caye and is an excellent spot for a night dive. Divers are greeted by octopus, basket starfish and trunkfishes. The trunkfishes are quite tame and can be held just long enough for your partner to take a photograph. The area is renowned for its crustaceans with lots of lobster, crab and shrimp.

59. MANTA REEF

Here from December to May, divers will find huge manta rays. A curious, lethargic creature known in many parts of the world as the devilfish, the manta ray has a grace and beauty all its own. These fish fly through the water in slow motion with a gentle, rhythmic undulation. On occasions they are seen in the distance leaping out of the water.

Like the whale shark, the manta ray appears to be unaware of divers. They simply do not perceive divers as a threat, and it is quite possible to hitch a ride on the back of one of these mighty titans. I have watched spellbound for what seemed like an eternity as two of these creatures staged an underwater ballet.

Large and colorful formations of tube sponges are particularly plentiful on the northeast side of Glovers Reef. Photo: Joe Miller.

This juvenile spotted drum will eventually grow spots on its tail and second (rear) dorsal fin. Its long first dorsal fin will shorten as it reaches maturity. Photo: Keith Ibsen.

Performing what was likely a pre-mating ritual, the pair approached each other head on. As they neared contact they rose up towards the surface in unison and continued over and backwards, each completing a full circle. They continued to swim around each other, always close but never making direct contact.

The slope here drops steeply from 40 feet to 200 feet (12-61 m). The water is exceptionally clear and the reef wall spectacular.

60. ELKHORN FOREST

This site is just north of Southwest Cayes and is excellent for either rounding off a busy day in shallow water, or a night dive. The corals here rate alongside the very best in Belize with elkhorn being the most abundant. For me, the best time to dive this site is just as it begins to get dark when the nocturnal fish are leaving their daytime refuge in order to seek food. Anyone who is familiar with this site in the daytime will see a complete transformation during the early hours of darkness. Divers will find octopus, a variety of starfish, spiny lobsters, and many varieties of crab and shrimp. In addition, divers are very likely to find a number of parrotfishes wrapped in protective cocoons of mucus as they rest for the night. The maximum depth is 25 feet (8 m).

61. DOLPHIN DANCE

Dolphins are regularly seen here all year round and regularly join divers underwater with their playful antics. Sometimes they are difficult to photograph because they are so close. The best tip I can offer is to try and hang back and allow other divers to interact with them. A wide-angle lens is essential for a dolphin shot.

62. HOLE IN THE WALL

Immediately south of Long Caye is a natural tunnel with coral growing on all sides. At the very top of the underwater ledge at a depth of just 50 feet (15 m), divers can enter a tunnel into another realm. Occasionally the hole is teeming with thousands of silversides which move gracefully to one side to allow unobstructed passage to the exit at a depth of 80 feet (24 m). Divers emerge on the face of the reef wall amidst a forest of large colorful gorgonians.

Parrotfishes come in many different sizes and colors, but are easily recognized by their beak-like mouths. This is the stoplight parrotfish. Photo: Keith Ibsen.

The sharksucker, a large member of the remora family, is usually found accompanying larger fish in order to gather scraps of food when the larger fish feeds. Occasionally, they follow divers or attach themselves to boats. Here a snorkeler entices a sharksucker with a handout off the Turneffe Islands. Photo: Keith Ibsen.

63. PARROTFISH FALLS

Just north of Long Caye on the very edge of the cut is a dive site which is a favorite of many divers. Famous for its parrotfishes, especially the blue and midnight, the underwater terrain is a dramatic collection of vertical walls and tunnels festooned with a wide variety of coral, including large specimens of giant brain coral. At the base of the wall, the coral breaks up as it comes into contact with the sand. Here divers will find one of my favorite marine creatures—the red-banded coral shrimp. There are also many nudibranchs and other minute life forms which offer great opportunities for macro photography.

64. LONG CAYE CUT

Between Long Caye and Northeast Caye is one of the four navigable channels through the reef. It is generally shallow, averaging about 30 feet (9 m), with a light distribution of coral and numerous sandy patches. Midnight, stoplight and blue parrotfish are abundant and are much tamer here than at many other locations where they tend to stay just far enough from divers to make photography difficult. It is not uncommon for the blue parrotfish to grow to almost 4 feet (12 m) here. Parrotfishes are always on the move and are interesting to watch as they grind coral with their parrot-like beaks, extracting the polyps and algae, and spewing out the sandy residue. Parrotfishes are present throughout the Caribbean, but nowhere have I seen them as large as at Parrotfish Falls and Long Caye Cut.

Caution. Divers must watch out for small boats using the cut. Fishermen do not always appreciate the problems encountered by divers and the water is shallow. Boat cover or, at the very least, a dive flag marker buoy towed by the diver is essential.

65. CHAPEL SPIRES

The next dive site to the north which is regularly visited is another one where the coral has formed into large pinnacles or spires rising up out of the seabed like a metropolis of high rises. In addition, some of the largest pieces of giant brain coral to be found anywhere in Belize are concentrated in this one location. Many divers will notice only the overall dark color of the coral as they swim past, yet each is slightly different and edged with delicate purples or perhaps a deep red. The coloring is a sure sign that these corals are in a very healthy state.

Young adult specimens of almost every variety of parrotfish are a particular feature here, although the diver will find almost all the common reef fishes at this very pretty dive site.

This site is just north of North Caye in the North Channel, and the same cautions about boat traffic apply as at Long Caye Cut.

66. SHARK POINT

Many local divers will testify that they see sharks on every dive at this particular spot. Caribbean reef, lemon and the occasional blacktip and bull are the most common varieties, with the oceanic whitetip putting in a rare appearance. A large grouper or jewfish would provide a good meal for a shark, and it is likely that the abundance of such fish at this corner of the atoll has something to do with the presence of so many sharks.

67. GROUPER POINT

The underwater ledge here at the northeast corner of the atoll is about 2 miles (3 km) wide at its widest. The depth of the ledge is fairly uniform at 60 to 70 feet (18-21 m). It is strewn with little pinnacles of coral topped with sea fans and gorgonians, and interspersed with scattered sand patches. During December and January, groupers spawn here in the thousands. Collecting in vast numbers along the ledge, they head for shallower waters inside the reef, paying little attention to divers. All members of the grouper family are here, both large and small. I cannot help but wonder where they all come from during the spawning season. A diver might find himself on a fairly barren stretch when, suddenly, groupers are everywhere. Like a swarm they rise up, almost in unison, and head in the same direction. During the remainder of the year, groupers and jewfish are present in good numbers.

68. QUEEN ANGEL POINT

Right below the reef crest at the northwest corner of the atoll, angelfishes are particularly common. Large French and gray angelfish are the most prominent, but the queen angelfish and the delightful rock beauty are also present in good numbers. This is the only place in Belize that I have seen the cherubfish, although it is quite common elsewhere in the Caribbean. The entire site from the beginning of the sheltered side of the reef is tremendous diving, with clear water and a wonderful variety of different corals.

Grouper Point is the spawning ground in December and January for large numbers of groupers such as this black grouper. Photo: Keith Ibsen.

The sleek beauty of the barracuda can sometimes be overlooked because of its unwarranted reputation. Photo: Ned Middleton.

Since local fishermen tend to work the eastern side of the Turneffe Islands, spiny lobsters are more readily found on the western side of the atoll. Photo: Keith Ibsen.

69. TURTLE TAVERN

Turtles are so common at this particular site that seeing at least one is virtually guaranteed. As many as five were seen on one dive and the species vary from day to day. The terrain comprises a gentle slope covered in coral with staghorn being the most prominent. There are plenty of juvenile fish and lots of small holes occupied by moray eels. The entire setting, which is only 30 feet (9 m) deep, is simply alive with marine life.

70. BLACK FOREST

This site is named after the amazing wall-to-wall covering of black coral. Throughout the world divers have to travel deeper and deeper in order to find both red coral (not a Caribbean species) and black coral because they are much sought after by the jewelry trade. The visiting diver will be shown this site by the tour guide and will not be permitted to remove any of the coral.

71. MASADA

Here a magnificent giant plateau of coral rises up from about 110 feet (33 m) almost to the surface. It is a beautiful creation of corals, tunnels, caves and swim-throughs. A marvelous variety of fishes, especially the smaller reef fishes, are everywhere. Red-banded coral shrimp, arrow crabs and spotted drums are found all around the atoll, but are more common around this entire plateau. However, a diver must look for them carefully in the many crevices.

72. CARGO SITE

Close to Masada is an area marked on the chart as a wreck site. To my knowledge there is no actual wreckage, but a large cruise liner did run aground at this point some years ago. Apparently, in order to lighten the ship, much of its load was jettisoned. The wine cellar was apparently part of the abandoned cargo for bottles of various liquors are still occasionally found. This site ranks as one of the few dives in the world where cocktails are the "catch of the day."

73. CATHEDRAL SPIRES

These are the largest and most spectacular spires I have ever seen. From 130 feet (39 m) they rise to a depth of 30 feet (9 m). These three separate pinnacles of coral-encrusted rock are truly magnificent constructions of nature. This entire southwest corner is the most protected part of the reef and is home to some of the prettiest diving to be found anywhere.

74. THE ANCHOR

This is one of the most curious anchors I have ever encountered. It sits at a depth of 168 feet (51 m), is a little over 6 feet (2 m) long and has a very thick stock—maybe as much as 18 inches (46 cm) in diameter. A chain lies across the reef, reaching up as far as 70 feet (21 m) from the surface. There is also a line going down in the opposite direction and out of sight. There is probably nothing tied to the end of that line, but some weighty object made it run straight down the reef face, and the thought of what that might have been conjures up all sorts of possibilities.

Large barrel sponges are very common throughout Belize. During the day many nocturnal animals take shelter in the large central cavity. Photo: Ned Middleton.

CHAPTER VIII LIGHTHOUSE REEF

REEF ROUNDUP

Of the three atoll reefs off the coast of Belize, Lighthouse Reef is the farthest offshore. It is far from neglected, however, since dive boats from San Pedro visit the atoll regularly and the larger live-aboard vessels are always found in the vicinity.

Within the confines of the reef, the depth is generally about 9 feet (2.7 m) with sufficient room between the numerous patch reefs to maneuver any craft with shallow enough draft. The seabed is sandy and this, at least, allows the skipper to see the darker-colored patches of coral. As long as the sun is over the shoulder, the patch reefs are clearly seen. However, as soon as you turn and face the sun, the glare from the surface obscures the coral and extreme caution is advised.

There are also six cayes. In the north, **Sandbore Caye** is one of the two cayes equipped with lighthouses occupied by a keeper and his family. Nearby is **Northern Caye** and these two cayes are known locally as **Northern Two Cayes**. On Northern Caye is one of the newest offshore diving resorts. Much of the caye has well-matured mangroves and there is an internal lagoon. The caye is noted for its saltwater crocodiles and snowy egrets.

Halfway down the west coast, there is a small caye called **White Pelican Caye**. The white pelican is not regarded as a species indigenous to Belize, so their being here is unusual. I first saw a large flock of these splendid birds in 1988, and have heard that they frequently stop at this point when in transit. Further south, there is **Long Caye**, which is a veritable jungle and home for far too many mosquitoes for reasonable comfort. However, some of the best diving is found to the west of Long Caye. The nutrients are pushed westward by the prevailing winds and there are no lagoons of fresh or brackish water to destroy the reef. Just below Long Caye is **Hat Caye** which is very small and inaccessible by boat.

The one remaining caye is possibly my favorite place on earth. **Half Moon Caye** sits at the lower southeast corner of the reef and is nothing short of paradise. This small, idyllic tropical island and the immediate surrounding waters are a National Park and home to a protected bird sanctuary. The caye is divided into two distinct halves: the western half is the bird sanctuary and is densely overgrown. The remainder of the island is made up of coconut palms and sparse vegetation, with a few small buildings and a solar-powered lighthouse.

The lighthouse keeper on Half Moon Caye has seen many divers come and go. He keeps a visitors book which most of them sign. In addition to making his living from fishing and his duties as lighthouse keeper, he is the park warden and keeps a close eye on all visitors. He has even built a platform amongst the trees, which enables visitors to view the birds from a position which looks down onto the treetops.

The nesting birds are mainly frigate and red-footed booby birds, but a total of 98 species have been recorded here: pelican, osprey, egret, gulls, storks and terns, to name but a

The shallow rim of the Great Blue Hole is profuse with marine life in contrast to the interior, where the walls are mostly bare and the waters devoid of fishes. Photo: Keith Ibsen.

Half Moon Caye is a protected bird
sanctuary where red-footed booby
birds (left) can be found nesting in
close proximity to frigate birds
(right). Their peaceful coexistence
ends during feeding time. The
frigate, with its seven-foot (2 m)
wingspan, tries to rob the returning
booby birds of their fish. Photos:
Ned Middleton.

few. Every day the frigate and booby birds put
on a remarkable social display. At first light
they can be seen soaring high above the island
as one large flock. With hardly any noticeable
wing movement, they ride the early morning
air currents. Later, during the intense heat of
the day, they can be easily photographed at
their nests from the viewing platform.
There is no obvious segregation in the nesting
arrangements. Each bird, irrespective of
species, has its own site. These are all very
close to each other, often no more than
pecking distance apart.

The magnificent frigate bird, to quote the full
name, is much larger than the booby bird. It
has a seven-foot wingspan and a much longer
beak. Every day it uses this advantage of size to
rob the booby bird of its food. By mid-
afternoon, when the heat from the sun is
diminishing, the booby birds go fishing. Like
many species of seabird found around the
world, it dives onto its prey from a great height
over the sea.

By contrast, the frigate bird never lands on
water, although it is very adept at plucking a
dead fish from the surface. The afternoon ritual
between these two species is one whereby the
booby bird runs a gauntlet of harassing frigate
birds which attempt, quite viciously, to make
the booby bird drop its catch. And so the truce
which had prevailed since last evening is
broken. One cannot help but will the booby
bird on to victory, and feel like cheering each
time one of them returns successfully to the
nest to live in peaceful coexistence with its
aggressor until the following afternoon.

LIGHTHOUSE REEF

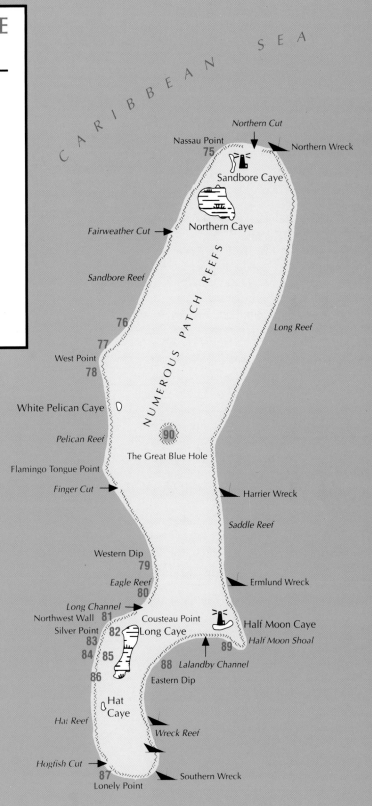

CARIBBEAN SEA

Northern Cut
Nassau Point
75
Northern Wreck
Sandbore Caye
Northern Caye
Fairweather Cut
Sandbore Reef
Long Reef
NUMEROUS PATCH REEFS
76
77
West Point
78
White Pelican Caye
90
Pelican Reef
The Great Blue Hole
Flamingo Tongue Point
Finger Cut
Harrier Wreck
Saddle Reef
Western Dip
79
Eagle Reef
80
Ermlund Wreck
Long Channel
Northwest Wall   81
Cousteau Point
Silver Point   Long Caye   Half Moon Caye
83   82
84   85   Half Moon Shoal
86   89
88   Lalandby Channel
Eastern Dip
Hat
Caye
Hat Reef
Wreck Reef
Hogfish Cut
87   Southern Wreck
Lonely Point

Admiralty Chart 959 also shows a **Saddle Caye** just to the north of Half Moon Caye, but this does not appear to exist anymore.

On the eastern side of Lighthouse Reef are six wrecks and these are clearly marked on the chart. From a distance, three of these look quite intact as they sit high and dry up on top of the reef. The largest of these vessels is about 1,000 yards (909 m) north of Half Moon Caye and dominates the scenery. The *Ermlund* was a total write-off in 1971. This ship of approximately 4,000 gross tons lost power during a storm and was deposited on the reef by a large wave.

Five miles (8 km) north is another vessel, which is a key landmark in locating the Great Blue Hole. Originally sitting intact on top of the reef, it was used by the RAF for target practice some years ago (a practice no longer allowed). The ship was literally split in two and moved some distance down the reef crest, initially causing great difficulty for navigators trying to find the entrance to the Great Blue Hole.

The ship has been given a number of uninspiring names over the years, such as **Broken in Two Wreck** or **Two Halves Wreck**. Recently, however, the wreck has succumbed further to the ravages of the relentless Caribbean swells and is now in at least three main sections. The best name that I have heard is **Harrier**, after the type of aircraft used by the RAF to target the vessel, and hereafter in this book it is called **Harrier Wreck**.

At the very north of the reef is one of the few substantial entrances through the reef crest. One ship, misjudging the entrance, foundered here during a storm. This **Northern Wreck** is well broken up with almost all the wreckage below the surface. Diveable, it is ideal for rounding off the day with the air remaining from the last dive. The entire wreckage is teeming with grunts. In the shallows, divers have to be careful not to be thrown about by the prevailing Caribbean swells.

South of Half Moon Caye are the other two wrecks which, from a distance, look intact. Although different in design they are similar in size. Relatively small, I would describe them as inshore cargo vessels.

Southern Wreck is located at the southern tip of the atoll and is very similar to Northern Wreck. The large engine block is still above

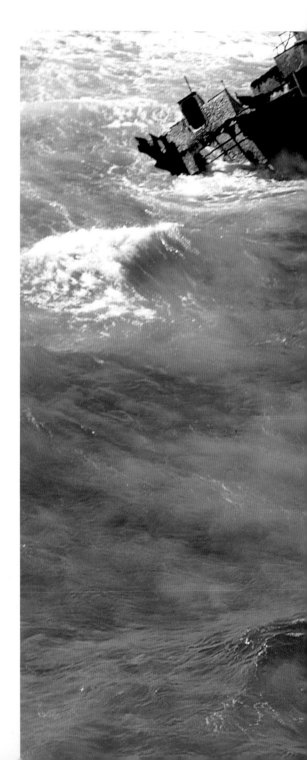

About 5 miles (8 km) north of the Ermlund is Harrier Wreck, so named because it was once used for Harrier bombing practice. It is from this wreck that bearings are taken to the Great Blue Hole. Photo: Ned Middleton.

Although the slipper lobster is dramatically different in appearance from its spiny relative, it is a lobster nonetheless. Photo: Keith Ibsen.

the surface, but the remainder of the wreckage is scattered far and wide, and has nothing to offer divers.

The entire circumference of Lighthouse Reef comprises coral which breaks the surface, forming a natural barrier against the sea. The prevailing winds and waves are from the northeast and, therefore, the calmer water is found along the western coast. Very few people dive the eastern coast of Lighthouse Reef, yet it is quite splendid and often spectacular.

On the east, **Saddle Reef** stretches from Half Moon Caye to **Harrier Wreck**. **Long Reef** then continues as far as **Northern Wreck**. This entire reef crest is dominated by staghorn, elkhorn and giant brain coral with many other varieties also present. This is one of the most extensive stretches of healthy and abundant coral in Belize. Sloping down rapidly at first from the surface, the reef continues down to about 40 feet (12 m) at a less severe rate. Here there is an underwater ledge, up to a half mile (.8 km) wide in places. It is to this ledge that the fishermen come from Belize City. In their small *teresita* sailing craft with holds full of ice, they catch grouper and jewfish of tremendous proportions on hand-held lines. The ledge slopes very gradually until the top of the drop-off is reached between 120 and 140 feet (36 and 42 m). The vertical drop continues down to depths of over 2,600 feet (788 m).

This is one of the most unexplored stretches of coastline in Belize, as the conditions are usually unfavorable for diving.

Northern Cut is one of only two substantial breaks in the reef. The underwater ledge is still very wide in this area and **Nassau Point** is another area where grouper like to spawn. Large Nassau grouper and rock hind are found all year round in the deeper waters, with countless snapper in the shallows.

The beautiful patterns of the flamingo tongue is actually the mantle of the mollusk and not its shell. Photo: Keith Ibsen.

Moving south along the western coast is **Sandbore Reef**. Here the continuous ledge begins to break up, and spur and groove formations begin to appear. The coral structures are, however, very impressive and rise up some 40 to 50 feet (12-15 m) above the sand chutes. There are many tunnels, small caves and swim-throughs which add to the overall dramatic effect.

Throughout the length of **Pelican Reef** to the south of Sandbore Reef, divers are confronted by endless varieties of coral to a depth of 30 feet (9 m) before encountering the wall. Tube and barrel sponges are common, and there is a good chance of seeing nurse and bull sharks.

At **Flamingo Tongue Point** gorgonians and sea fans adorn the coral compositions. On many of these, flamingo tongue cowries are found, usually in pairs. This is a delightful little shellfish which is easy to photograph as it grazes slowly along the gorgonian stalks. Many divers have collected these shells only to discover that the beautiful spots disappear when the animal dies as they are not on the shell, but are part of the retractable mantle.

Underwater the spur and groove configurations continue as far as **Cousteau Point**. The large coral heads remain exciting and contain many creatures which divers might see for the first time.

There are few breaks through the reef crest north of **Long Channel**. Two that are used by the diving trade are **Fairweather Cut** and **Finger Cut**. Both are very narrow and can only be found by those with detailed knowledge of the reef.

Along **Western Dip** the design of the ledge begins to take on a more continuous look with the spurs becoming much wider and the sand chutes very narrow. The ledge eventually becomes unbroken just before the dive site called the Corner. From a depth of 40 feet (12 m) the reef wall is vertical, becoming more gradual at depths of 100 to 120 feet (30-36 m). Bull and nurse sharks are regular visitors, as are manta and spotted eagle rays.

Continuing south are rich and colorful coral structures at the very edge of a precipitous drop-off which are a feature of almost the entire length of **Hat Reef**. Each group of corals creates a unique arrangement. While each is very different, they all are worthy of attention.

South of **Silver Point**, the drop-off continues

to enthrall. Elkhorn and staghorn corals peer over the top of the barrel and tube sponges which adorn the wall. Brain corals and mountainous star corals compete with each other to cover the reef wall while at the same time providing an anchorage for tunicates of all shapes and sizes. Hammerhead sharks have been seen cruising the reef, but these encounters are rare. It is more likely that divers will confront nurse sharks, spotted eagle rays or very large barracuda.

From **Lonely Point** north along **Wreck Reef**, the underwater ledge is wider and very similar to the ledge north of Half Moon Caye. Queen conch are found here, but oddly enough, I have not found any areas of sea grass on which it is so dependent for food. Once again the area is constantly buffeted by the Caribbean and is unsuitable for diving except on the calmest of days. When conditions are right, however, it can be a most rewarding experience with sightings of some of the larger pelagics.

From **Eastern Dip** all the way to **Half Moon Shoal**, the south-facing reef compositions are as exciting as anywhere else in Belize and very popular among divers. With the winds and waves originating from the northeast, nature has created a unique, sheltered spot on the eastern coast.

SPECIFIC DIVE SITES

Listed below is a selection of some of the best dive sites on Lighthouse Reef.

75. GORGONIAN FOREST

The entire northwest corner of the atoll offers underwater visibility at its best, and the terrain below the surface is truly magnificent. The massive coral outcrops rising up from the ledge at the very edge of the precipice are covered in a splendid gorgonian forest. The "foliage" ranges from the palest pinks and greens to the deepest reds and darkest blues and purples. Some of the finest examples of reef fishes in their prime are found here in good numbers.

Tarpon Wall boasts fascinating clusters of sponges. When diving any wall, glance occasionally towards the open ocean where pelagics can often be seen. Photo: Keith Ibsen.

76. THE PLAYGROUND

The Playground begins as a fairly featureless, sandy course sloping gently down to a depth of about 50 feet (15 m). Here a vertical wall drops to a narrow ledge at 100 feet (30 m). At the very limit of this ledge the coral rises up like a wide fence, some 25 to 30 feet (8-9 m) high on the far side of which is the final drop-off. This curious profile is full of big lobster, while fish life is abundant at every depth level.

77. TRES CABEZA

Just north of West Point is a bare, rocky outcrop. About 100 yards (91 m) due west of this marker at a depth of 30 feet (9 m) is Tres Cabeza, meaning "three heads." Here one encounters three large and magnificent coral structures. They provide countless hideaways for grouper and lobster. Turtles are regularly seen here and there is good chance of seeing manta and large spotted eagle rays.

78. TARPON WALL

Just below West Point is Tarpon Wall with a distinctive profile all its own. The sandy ledge drops gently to a depth of 35 feet (11 m) over a distance of about 100 yards (91 m). Here the coral has formed another barrier and rises up to within 15 feet (5 m) of the surface. On the far side of this barrier is a 75-foot (23 m) vertical drop to a narrow ledge at a depth of 90 feet (27 m). Beyond this ledge the reef wall continues its vertical descent. Lobster, grouper and snapper fill the many tunnels and small schools of jacks and tarpon can be expected on every dive.

The Northwest Wall begins at The Corner. This is a good place to see spotted eagle rays. Photo: Ned Middleton.

79. MANTA WALL

This site is well known for its manta rays which are often seen leaping out of the water in the distance—an impressive spectacle. The wall is rife with other intriguing marine life as well, which on one occasion had occupied the last frames of my film when I turned to see what seemed like a monstrous apparition—a huge albino manta ray. Thus you'll just have to take me at my word on this.

80. EAGLE REEF

Long Channel is the main entrance to the atoll and is continually used by small craft. Just north of this channel, west of the reef crest known as Eagle Reef, there is some spectacular diving. However, the diver must always be aware of the surface traffic. Diving here is best later in the day when the sunlight penetrates to greater depths. The underwater ledge is narrow and covered in an abundance of coral, especially black coral. All the reef fishes are present along with some splendid grouper and snapper. This is where we begin to find small groups of the very largest spotted eagle rays cruising the reef.

81. THE CORNER

The Corner is the beginning of the Northwest Wall. The scenery as seen from 30 feet (9 m) above this living vertical wall is as sensational as anywhere else in the Caribbean. Manta rays are still seen, but the small groups of large spotted eagle rays are ever present. Single large barracuda hover almost unnoticed in these well-chosen hunting grounds. At the top of the cliff face, large angelfishes abound, and in the deeper waters the grouper are always ready to confront the diver with a challenging stare.

Hermit crabs use empty shells for their homes. As they grow they will move to progressively larger shells. Photo: Keith Ibsen.

82. THE "V'S"

Here at a depth of 30 feet (9 m), divers are above a narrow ledge, looking down on a magnificent reef wall which continues unbroken for some distance around a complex and very interesting part of the coastline. This site is named after the V-shaped coral formations at the top of the wall.

83. THE ZOO

This site is so named because of the tremendous variety of fish in a single spot. All the common reef fishes are not only here, and in good numbers, they are each a splendid example of the species. Along the ledge above the reef wall, the corals are arranged in tidy little combinations, each being attractive to a particular species. Sergeant major damselfish will occupy one coral head with the blue chromis firmly inhabiting another. Below them the longspine squirrelfish and rock beauty seek refuge in the large holes. All around, French angelfish, gray angelfish, banded butterflyfish and foureye butterflyfish flit from coral head to coral head—always in pairs. The very edge of the reef is at 30 feet (10 m) and below this, the wall is as equally exciting in terms of fish life.

84. SILVER CAVES

Like Silver Point, this site takes its name from a wealth of small silverside minnows. Countless numbers, perhaps even millions, of these small fish swim in such tight formations that they obscure the reef. Quite often the shoals will be attacked by hungry jacks and other predators— all very good for divers with underwater video equipment. As a diver swims through this avalanche of fish, they open in unison and the diver enters a tunnel of living fish which parts ahead of him and closes the door behind him. Like all shoals they move in perfect harmony, as though obeying a single command inaudible to the human ear.

It is above this stretch of reef that some of the larger live-aboard dive boats anchor. The depth here is never more than 20 to 25 feet (6-8 m) above the ledge.

85. CATHEDRAL

At this point the ledge is very wide and contains a veritable catalog of the most exquisite fishes and marine creatures. Moray eels, especially green moray, are fairly common. Right in the center of the site is a tall arrangement of corals which rise like a small cluster of church spires. The tallest of these is over 8 feet (2.4 m) tall.

Between Silver Caves and Cathedral at the top of the reef wall, I witnessed a curious mating spectacle. Numerous creole wrasse were swimming around in pairs. Altogether there were thousands of these fish, but each pair was swimming independently. The male would swim above and behind the larger female. The fish were swimming with their pectoral fins, causing an erratic, almost comical, motion as they engaged in this ritual.

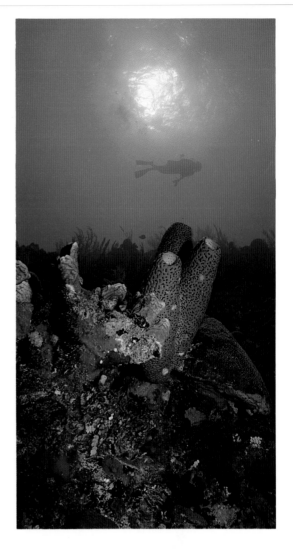

Many colorful varieties of sponges thrive in Belizean waters. Photo: Joe Miller.

Silverside minnows move in perfect symmetry at Silver Point and Silver Caves where they are particularly prevalent. Photo: Joe Miller.

86. QUEBRADA

South of Cathedral is Quebrada (the break), a single sand chute through the coral which reaches all the way to the reef wall. This wide ledge in such shallow water is absolutely amazing. The corridor allows divers to swim along inspecting the marine life which hides at the bottom of the coral. Arrow crabs, red-banded coral shrimp and juvenile spotted drums are all there, as well as a good number of green moray eels.

87. HOGFISH CUT

Towards Hogfish Cut the continuous coral ledge begins to break up and the gaps between each coral head become very wide. Large hogfish are found here in significant numbers. The male, which can grow up to 3 feet (1 m) long, is a contrasting, almost black and white fish with three long spines at the beginning of the dorsal fin. It is shy and often difficult to photograph.

88. FLATS WALL

Right in the middle of Eastern Dip there is a little-known cut through the reef crest. No more than 15 feet (5 m) wide, it is an entrance to be used only by those who know the area well. Below this cut is a curious dive site known as Flats Wall. From the reef crest the bedrock slopes gently and consistently away to a depth of 45 to 50 feet (14-15 m) at the top of the drop-off.

This bedrock is covered in conch grass. One assumes from the name that the conch feed on this grass as well as sea grass, but no conch were seen on my visits to the site. Conch grass is different from sea grass; it looks like a covering of green moss and definitely attracts a number of different minute creatures. Hydrozoans, tunicates, small crabs and shrimp take the place of the common reef fishes, although a small number are always present. Large sea fans and gorgonians dominate the edge of the ledge.

89. HALF MOON WALL

The reef crest comprises a veritable thicket of staghorn coral with other corals also present. The reef drops steeply to a shelf at a depth of about 15 feet (5 m). Along this shelf there is a large expanse of sand which at first glance appears totally uninteresting. It is here, however, that a large community of garden eels is found. From a distance divers will think they are looking at sparse vegetation, but on closer examination each "leaf" turns out to be the upper half of a small eel protruding upright from its hole in the sand. A diver may get as close as 10 to 15 feet (3-5 m) before they all disappear from sight. Also known as sand eels, there are very few colonies of this mysterious little creature found in Belize, and none allow divers to venture too close.

The sand continues to slope gently until reaching a depth of between 45 and 50 feet (14-15 m). Here divers are at the back of Half Moon Wall, facing an outcrop of coral which rises up like a barrier along the very edge of the reef wall. To reach the front of the wall, you can rise up to within 20 feet (6 m) of the surface and swim over the barrier. There are also narrow gaps between the splendid outcrops of coral just wide enough for a single diver. The most interesting route is, as always, to find a tunnel and swim through the archway of living coral. Whichever route is taken, it is nothing compared to the breathtaking scenery which awaits.

Half Moon Wall is incredible. The vertical wall at times cuts back in on itself, displaying many interesting features. Sponges protrude at right angles to the reef, competing for space with gorgonians and sea fans. Mountainous star and giant brain coral are interspersed with smaller clumps of staghorn, brain and lettuce coral. Anchored amongst these are the hydrozoans and tunicates.

The top of the wall is ablaze with fish life: large angelfishes in groups of four or five; every variety of butterflyfish, always in pairs; large squirrelfishes posing outside their holes; and small grouper, impatient to see the world deeper down, looking and behaving in the same way as their much larger parents.

This intermediate blue tang will turn a dark blue as it becomes an adult. Tangs usually travel in small schools and are often accompanied by trumpetfishes. Photo: Keith Ibsen.

Turtles are common—they lay their eggs on Half Moon Caye—but the real excitement is generated by the pelagics. This is the only sheltered dive site on the eastern side of any of the three atoll reefs and divers can expect some really amazing encounters. Oceanic whitetip sharks (complete with their attendant pilotfish), lemon, blacktip and bull sharks are likely to be seen. The very largest of manta rays and good specimens of spotted eagle rays are frequently seen. At the very limit of safe diving are very large jewfish—some so large they might stalk the diver, although they pose no danger. The wall continues down well beyond the safe reach of scuba divers.

This magnificent site is only a short distance from the idyllic tropical island of Half Moon Caye, and combines marine and terrestrial beauty in a manner which is, in my experience, unsurpassed.

90. THE GREAT BLUE HOLE

Having circumnavigated the atoll reef, it is time to turn to one of the most astounding dive sites to be found anywhere on earth. Right in the center of Lighthouse Reef is a large, almost perfectly circular hole approximately one quarter of a mile (.4 km) across. Inside this hole the water is 480 feet (145 m) deep and it is the depth of water which gives the deep blue color that causes such structures throughout the world to be known as "blue holes."

In 1972, Jacques Cousteau took his famous research ship, *Calypso* into the Blue Hole, pioneering a route that is still used by the dive trade today. There were two popular rumors that sprang up regarding Cousteau's visit. The first was that Cousteau used explosives to blast a path through the atoll to reach the Blue Hole. This is not true. The second rumor was that Philippe Cousteau lost his life in the Blue Hole during that trip. This is nonsense. Philippe was killed when his aircraft—a converted Catalina —came in to land in Lisbon, Portugal a few years later.

Almost all the divers who visit Belize are keen to add this splendid dive site to their list of conquests. When they understand what the hole is and how it was formed, it makes the dive all the more exciting. The Blue Hole is a "karst-eroded sinkhole." It was once a cave at the center of an underground tunnel complex whose ceiling collapsed. Some of the tunnels are thought to be linked right through to the mainland, though this has never been conclusively proved. The mainland itself has many water-filled sinkholes that are connected to caves and tunnels.

At some time many millions of years ago, two distinct events occurred. First, there was a major earthquake and this probably caused the cave ceiling to collapse forming the sinkhole. The upheaval, however, had the effect of tilting Lighthouse Reef to an angle of around 12 degrees. All along the walls of this former cavern are overhangs and ledges, housing pleistocene stalactites, stalagmites and columns.

Some of the stalactites now hang at an angle, yet we know they cannot develop at any angle other than perfectly perpendicular. In addition, there are those stalactites which were formed after the earthquake and others which were formed both before and after that cataclysmic event—the top of the stalactite being at an angle and the bottom being perpendicular.

This limestone column is at a depth of 150 feet (50 m) inside the Great Blue Hole. Columns are formed when stalactites and stalagmites meet and create a single structure. Photo: Ned Middleton.

The Great Blue Hole's stalactites are a reminder that this spectacular dive site was once a dry cave. Photo: Joe Miller.

At that time the sea levels were much lower than today and the second major event was to change all this. At the end of the Great Ice Age the glaciers melted and sea levels throughout the world rose considerably. This process occurred in stages. Evidence for this are the shelves and ledges, carved into the limestone by the sea, which run the complete interior circumference of the Blue Hole at various depths. The first of these ledges is found between 150 and 165 feet (45-50 m) and is best visited on the south side. The base of the ledge is perfectly flat and cuts back into the rock some 15 to 20 feet (5-6 m). This creates an ever-narrowing cavern until the roof reaches the floor right at the back. Here in the V-shaped ledges, cut into solid limestone, are stalactites, stalagmites and columns (where stalactites and stalagmites have joined) which do not exist in the shallower waters of the Blue Hole.

There is very little marine life in the hole, and the walls are of bare rock largeiy due to the scarcity of direct sunlight on the walls, but this hardly matters. Occasionally a lone hammerhead shark is seen, but the general lack of fish, and therefore food, suggests that the creature was simply passing through. The only other fish I have seen were four pompano, but other species have been seen, especially on the south side. Lemon and blacktip sharks, and horse-eyed jacks are spotted with some regularity.

Diving the Blue Hole is not for beginners, although anyone can complete a shallow dive and claim to have dived this marvelous wonder of nature. The deeper one dives into the Blue Hole, the clearer the water and the more breathtaking the scenery. But diving deeper than sport diving depths is for specialists only and cave diving requires even more training and equipment. This type of diving is not generally available in Belize, but a few groups have visited the Blue Hole in order to explore the tunnels and caves which extend from within. On the western side at a depth of 230 feet (70 m), there is an entrance through a narrow tunnel into a large cavern. In total darkness the stalactites, stalagmites and columns exist in an undisturbed world. The floor is covered with a very fine silt which billows into great clouds with the slightest movement from a passing diver. In the farthest corner, another narrow tunnel leads upwards into a second cavern and then another leads finally to a third cavern. Here are the skeletal remains of turtles which found their way in but never found their way out. This is the very danger which faces a diver. Now at a depth of only 100 feet (30 m) he must find his way back by the same route down to 230 feet (70 m) before he can commence his surfacing and decompression schedule. If he, his buddy or even a turtle have stirred up the silt, the chances are he will never find his way out again. For those qualified cave divers, this is a very rewarding dive.

The Great Blue Hole is not marked on Admiralty Charts—the task of a survey ship is to map that portion of reef which represents a danger to shipping. The hole is found almost exactly in the center of the reef on a course of 330° from Harrier Wreck. For me, an entire diving trip to Belize is worth the effort and expense for this single dive.

Divers should be observant to avoid coming in contact with the spines of sea urchins. Photo: Ned Middleton.

The large West Indian sea star is often found in turtle grass beds. Because of its popularity with collectors it is now hard to find. Photo: Ned Middleton.

CHAPTER IX   BANCO CHINCHORRO

Mexico

REEF ROUNDUP

Even with only a quick glance at the chart, the experienced eye of the wreck diver is immediately drawn to one particular atoll reef—Banco Chinchorro.

Chinchorro is just to the north of Belize inside the territorial waters of Mexico, and because of its archaeological importance, is protected by Mexican law. Ships have been running aground on Chinchorro since man first made some form of rude craft and went to sea. Many modern steel wrecks are evident, but Spanish galleons have also been discovered and partially excavated. One particular site harbored over 40 cannon until one enterprising individual decided to remove them all for himself. He was later arrested.

For trips to Banco Chinchorro, I have chartered the *Reef Roamer II*, which operates out of San Pedro. When traveling to a foreign country by boat you are required to visit a recognized port of entry. In our case this was Xcalak, a small village which was decimated by a hurricane in the 1950's and has never recovered. Before that storm, over 3,500 people lived in Xcalak and it was an important copra-producing area, with roads and a communications system suitable for an industrial region. Today there are only a few hundred villagers.

Although Chinchorro is protected by law, we were still allowed to dive the atoll as long as we observed a few strict regulations. We were not permitted to touch or remove any wreckage, coral or shells. In addition, we were required to pay for a local guide to accompany

Trumpetfishes often await their prey while suspended upside down among gorgonian sea whips. Photo: Joe Miller.

Special arrangements need to be made to visit Banco Chinchorro since it lies inside Mexican waters. Dive boats such as the Reef Roamer II are available for charter. Photo: Ned Middleton.

the trip. In other words, we were allowed to take photographs and leave bubbles, and someone came along to ensure we did exactly that.

Inside the reef the water is 10 to 15 feet (3-5 m) deep. There are three cayes: **Cayo Norte**, **Cayo Centro** and **Cayo Lobos**, with Cayo Centro being the largest. The remainder of the shallow area within the reef is made up of several patch reefs which present a danger to ships seeking shelter.

About 3 miles (5 km) north of Cayo Lobos are the largely intact remains of the **SS Far Star**, where we witnessed a strange feeding phenomenon that I had never seen before, and the spectacle had me spellbound. The ship had struck the reef close to where two spurs jutted out from the main reef. One of these reached out to the left (facing the sea) at an angle of about 45 degrees and the other stretched out to

the right at about the same angle. This created a natural V-shaped fish trap. Seven large jewfish were herding a shoal of small silvery blue runners into this trap. The jewfish were spaced about 12 to 15 feet (4-5 m) apart, covering the large exit from the reef. As each fish took its turn to move in and feed from the milling shoal, the remainder would change position to keep the shoal within the trap.

On many occasions I have listened to the stories of divers who claim to know the wrecks of Chinchorro. In one place, I was told, there are three steel ships underwater lying one on top of the other! Other wrecks sit upright and virtually intact on the seabed. Unfortunately, I had been unable to find a guide who knows how to locate these wrecks, so on each of my visits we conducted a certain amount of searching.

Generally, the sea state on the northern and

BANCO CHINCHORRO

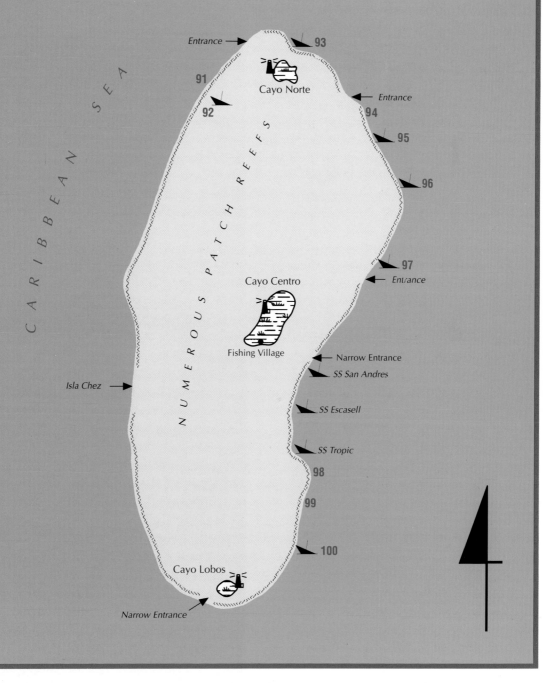

Entrance → 93

CARIBBEAN SEA

91

Cayo Norte

← Entrance

92

94

95

NUMEROUS PATCH REEFS

96

97

← Entrance

Cayo Centro

Fishing Village

← Narrow Entrance

SS San Andres

Isla Chez →

SS Escasell

SS Tropic

98

99

100

Cayo Lobos

Narrow Entrance

northwestern coast does not allow diving because the coastline is extremely exposed. It is that very exposure which makes the reef dangerous to shipping and, therefore, of interest to the wreck diver. Near Cayo Norte are two entrances through the reef. It seemed to me that at some time in the past there was every possibility of a ship failing to get through one of these gaps in a bid to find sheltered water. We selected a point between these two gaps and dropped down onto a ledge about 30 to 40 feet (9-12 m) deep. We swam along this ledge in a westerly direction. At first I was disappointed: the underwater terrain at this point is such that any vessel hitting the reef would have dropped into very deep water. Certainly the ledge was not wide enough to support a large wreck. At one point, just before reaching the actual gap in the reef, there is a large coral promontory—the most likely place for any ship to founder if it failed to reach the gap.

On the second dive of the day, in the late afternoon, we were approaching the promontory when we found the **Mystery Wreck**. There was only a short time remaining, but our intention was to return to the wreck on the following day. During that short time I was able to scan almost the entire port side of the vessel. I would estimate that the ship was a former steamer of approximately 1,500 gross tons. The bridge was situated at the stern with the remnants of cargo hatches forward of this position. Brass fittings, portholes and other paraphernalia were all still in place, which would indicate that this ship had never been salvaged. The ship was certainly not marked on the chart.

It appeared that the ship had hit the coral, probably becoming firmly wedged as the water poured in, and settled by the stern. The stern, looming up from beyond a depth of 100 feet (30 m), looked completely intact. The bow rests in about 20 feet (6 m) of water and is well broken up. The entire ship points upwards towards the surface as if making a last defiant gesture. Successive storms and the wave action have taken their toll on the shallower portion of the wreck.

Our skipper found a safe passage through the reef and we anchored for the night. Our dive team was excited at the prospect of exploring and photographing a large, almost intact

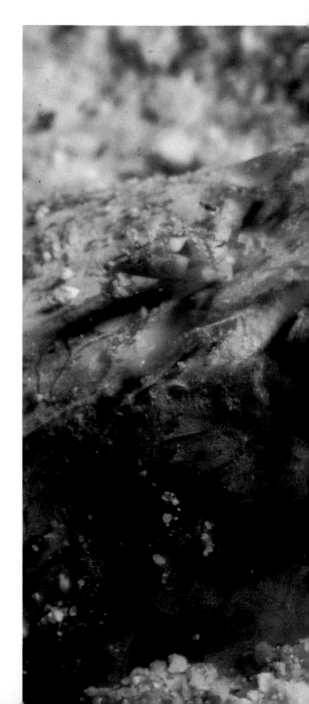

The sand diver seems aptly named as it awaits its unsuspecting prey on the sandy bottom. Photo: Keith Ibsen.

The delicate latticework of this gorgonian represents many years of growth. Photo: Ned Middleton.

Banco Chinchorro, the Mexican atoll to the north of Belize, is the final resting place for numerous shipwrecks, many of which are uncharted and unidentified. Photo: Ned Middleton.

shipwreck on the following day, but it was not to be. The weather changed and the rough sea along this stretch of the coast made diving impossible. We never did return to that wreck.

Banco Chinchorro is wild and bleak on the surface. Underwater the flora and fauna is not as rich and colorful as any of the three atolls in Belize, so the only reason to travel to Chinchorro is for the wrecks—if you can find them.

There are many more wrecks to be dived on Banco Chinchorro than the ones I have listed here, and its designation as a protected zone should help ensure exciting diving in the future. Chinchorro retains a quality of

spectacular wilderness because of the total absence of dive resorts and other charter boats. If anything goes wrong, you are a long way from home with little prospect of immediate assistance, so preparation is important. It is essential to have a guide with an intimate knowledge of the Chinchorro wrecks. The hotel and diving trade in Xcalak is in its infancy and consequently there were no local divers on whose experience I could draw. This means that Belize is the best route to Banco Chinchorro for the time being.

The flamingo tongue cowrie feeds on various corals, scooping out the polyps with its abrasive tongue. Photo: Ned Middleton.

The abundance of recognizable parts on a virgin shipwreck is a special bonus for an already exciting adventure. Photo: Ned Middleton.

Specific Dive Sites

91. SPANISH GALLEON NUMBER 1

Situated on the northwest corner of the atoll is the only wreck of which I am aware that lies on the western shore. Many wooden spars and struts lie loosely on the seabed at a depth of 15 to 20 feet (5-6 m) with approximately 30 iron cannon, countless cannon balls and ballast stones.

One of seven species of angelfishes found in Caribbean waters, the gray angelfish is easily approached. Photo: Ned Middleton.

92. SS CALDERA

This wreck is an interesting shallow dive on the inside edge of the reef. Several years ago the *SS Caldera* was running south before a storm and attempted to get inside the reef by running through the gap at full speed. The captain actually made it inside the reef before striking a patch reef and sinking. The wreck is now well broken up, but the boilers can still be seen above the surface. Underwater, there is a lot to explore as the wreckage is spread over a large area. This is a good site for a second or third dive of the day as the maximum depth is only 25 feet (8 m). There are quite a few angelfishes, butterflyfishes and damselfishes, and there is every likelihood of finding large spiny lobsters amongst the wreckage.

93. THE MYSTERY WRECK

As I described at the beginning of this chapter, this wreck is worth looking for again and is presumably still largely unexplored.

94. SPANISH GALLEON ANCHORS

At a depth of 10 feet (3 m) on the northeast corner of the reef are two large anchors. These have been identified as 15th or 16th century anchors of Spanish origin. It is possible that another, as yet undiscovered, Spanish galleon is wrecked nearby.

95. SS PENELOPEZ

The *SS Penelopez* was a steel boat about 50 feet (15 m) long which now lies in very shallow water on the inside edge of the reef. The wreck is too shallow for diving, however, the underwater terrain to the immediate east of the wreck is interesting. A wide ledge at a depth of 40 to 60 feet (12-18 m) is corrugated with long, wide fingers of rock festooned with gorgonians of all colors. In between these fingers, the sandy bottom provides home to countless large stingrays. Spotted eagle rays and turtles populate the entire area.

96. SS GINGER SCREW

A large vessel of about 8,000 gross tons, the *SS Ginger Screw* was carrying a full load of machinery, cars, trucks, jeans and juke boxes when she went down. The entire seabed over a very large area is littered with wreckage, although the wreck has been salvaged and little of the cargo, apart from some boxes of jeans, remains to be found. The wreck lies in 50 to 60 feet (15-18 m) and this allows divers plenty of time on the site. This is an excellent spot for exploring, and large spiny lobsters can often be found hiding amongst the wreckage.

97. SS GLEN VIEW

To the northeast of Cayo Centro there is a structure which, from a distance, looks like an oil rig. In reality it is the *SS Glen View*, a ship of about 4,000 gross tons with the bridge amidships. Both the stern section and most of the bow section are missing, leaving the center section, complete with bridge, high and dry on the reef. Apparently this particular wreck was a classic case of insurance write-off. Several years ago the local fishermen watched as the ship approached the coast cautiously, then turned and headed out to sea for about 5 miles (8 km) before turning once again and heading straight for the reef at full speed. The stern section, complete with two very large propellers, lies in shallow water just below the main hulk. There are lots of gorgonians, and large shoals of grunts and blue tang all swaying together in the shallow swells. The depth is so shallow that diving can be made difficult by the surface wave action. The wreck stretches from above the surface down to a maximum depth of 30 feet (9 m).

98. SPANISH GALLEON NUMBER 2

Never before have I seen a Spanish galleon, or any other wreck for that matter, laid out in this fashion. Wooden spars and struts lie loosely on the seabed like model parts laid out for assembly. Once again it is a shallow dive with a depth of only 15 to 20 feet (5-6 m). Sprinkled throughout the wreckage are iron cannon, cannon balls and ballast stones. The wreck is difficult to find without a guide as there are no obvious surface clues to its existence. It is important not to disturb the wreckage so that it may be properly surveyed at some time in the future.

99. STEEL PLATES

Just north of the *SS Uva* we found, almost by accident, a large number of steel plates clearly belonging to a large vessel whose name we were unable to discover. There was not a lot of wreckage, but it is a clear indication that a large wreck must be nearby. The area is certainly worth a search if you have the time.

100. *SS FAR STAR*

We nicknamed this site **The Mast** for the protruding mast by which we discovered the wreck. All of the wreckage is within 30 feet (9 m) of the surface. Not as spectacular as the Mystery Wreck, it is nonetheless an interesting dive with many swim-throughs and plenty of debris to keep the inquisitive diver busy. Large pieces of wreckage are spread over a considerable area. We found the anchors and chains, brass fittings, the engine room and a complete range of items associated with a ship that has never been salvaged. Certainly several years of winter storms and rough seas have taken their toll, but nothing else has interfered with this ship. We saw peacock flounder and plenty of large parrotfishes, especially the midnight.

Some wrecks are easier to find than others. Below this protruding mast lay the broken and scattered remains of the SS Far Star. Photos: Ned Middleton.

CHAPTER **X**   MARINE LIFE

There are far more fishes and invertebrates to be found off the coast of Belize than it is possible to include here. Those selected below are representative of the species most divers will see in Belize.

INTERESTING MARINE LIFE

Angelfishes

There are seven species of angelfishes found throughout the Caribbean. The smallest of these is the **cherubfish** (*Centropyge argi*) which is extremely rare. Angelfishes are frequently found in mated pairs and feed largely on sponges. Color patterns change markedly with maturity.

The **queen angelfish** (*Holocanthus ciliaris*) and **blue angelfish** (*Holocanthus bermudensis*) are very similar in appearance and often interchanged. The adult queen angelfish is actually bluer than the blue, and has a distinctive round blue "crown" above the forehead with yellow pectoral fins and tail. The blue has blue pectoral fins tipped in yellow, as is the tail. Adults grow up to 18 inches (46 cm) long and the juveniles of both species are almost identical. However, I have never seen the blue angelfish in Belize.

The **rock beauty** (*Holocanthus tricolor*) is a strikingly beautiful yellow and black fish which grows to about a foot (31 cm). It is quite common but is relatively shy.

The **French angelfish** (*Pomacanthus paru*) and **gray angelfish** (*Pomacanthus arcuatus*) are the most common of the entire family. The French is black with yellow spots and a rounded tail, and can grow up to 18 inches (46 cm). The gray is indeed gray with a straight-edged, blue-tipped tail and grows up to 2 feet (62 cm). These fish can be hand-fed and will approach divers for more food on successive dives in the same area.

Barracuda

Despite their undeserved fierce reputation, any injury from a **great barracuda** (*Sphyraena barracuda*) is likely to be the result of either catching one (by spear or line fishing) or from eating one. The barracuda has the dubious distinction of having caused more fish poisoning than any other fish. It is a beautiful, sleek silver fish which is extremely common. They are often seen in groups of similar size which thin out as they grow. The larger specimens, which can grow up to 6 feet (2 m) long, will have survived many spears and fishing lines, and will be solitary figures.

Butterflyfishes

Of five species of butterflyfishes found throughout the Caribbean, all are common in Belize except for the **longsnout butterflyfish** (*Prognathodes aculeatus*) which is rarely seen. All species are able to darken their body color at night.

Atlantic spadefish often form large schools and prefer a diet of shellfish. Photo: Joe Miller.

The **banded butterflyfish** (*Chaetodon striatus*), like most butterflyfishes, is usually found in pairs. It can grow to 6 inches (15 cm), and is found amongst corals in shallow waters.

The **foureye butterflyfish** (*Chaetodon capistratus*) has a spot near the tail, which can confuse would-be predators as to its size and orientation.

Crevalle Jacks

Crevalle jacks (*Caranx hippos*) are fast, and are a good game fish. They are also good for eating. The larger specimens, however, can be poisonous to eat. They grow to over 3 feet (1 m), and are usually spotted in the distance in small groups. They are often difficult to approach closely enough to photograph.

The vibrant blue chromis, a damselfish, can often been seen partnered with its duller brown relative, the brown chromis. Photo: Keith Ibsen.

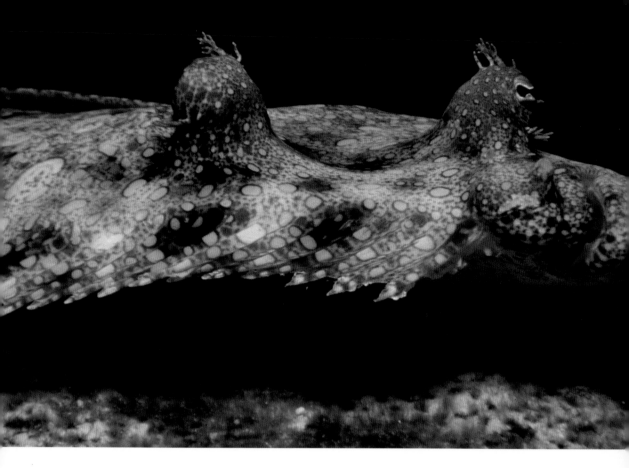

Although fairly common in Belize's waters, the peacock flounder often changes its bright blue coloring to blend in with its surroundings and can be easily overlooked. Photo: Keith Ibsen.

Damselfishes

Damselfishes are small and fiercely territorial. They have been known to dart out and nip at large fish and even divers when their space is violated. The female lays large clusters of reddish purple eggs which are guarded by the male until they hatch. He may produce chirping sounds when threatened.

The **sergeant major** (*Abudefduf saxatilis*) is easy to identify with its vertical black bars. Extremely common throughout Belize, they can lighten or darken their color to suit the surroundings. They grow up to 5 inches (13 cm).

The body colors of the **yellowtail damselfish** (*Microspathodon chrysurus*) may vary, but the small iridescent blue spots and the yellow tail can be easily identified. Juveniles usually have white tails.

Flounders

The **peacock flounder** (*Bothus lunatus*) is rather common, but is not often seen because of its superior camouflage. It can grow to 18 inches (46 cm), and the bright blue circles and spots on its tan body can quickly fade to blend with the background. Shortly after hatching, as with all flatfishes, one eye migrates towards the other and the fish becomes "sided." The flounder covers itself with sand, leaving only its eyes protruding while it awaits unsuspecting prey.

Some species of groupers can grow quite large. This Nassau grouper may grow to a length of 4 feet (1.2 m). Photo: Ned Middleton.

Groupers

Groupers are medium- to very large-sized sea basses. They lurk about holes in the reef near the bottom, catching smaller fishes in their big mouths with a sudden rush.

The **jewfish** (*Epinephalus itajara*), particularly common in Belize, can grow up to 8 feet (2.4 m) and weigh over 700 pounds (318 kg). It is a good fish for eating but, as is common throughout the Caribbean, the larger specimens can contain poisonous toxins. The locals catch these fish in great quantities around Lighthouse Reef. The bigger the fish the deeper the divers will have to descend in order to find it.

The **tiger grouper** (*Mycteroperca tigris*) is aptly named for its markings. This is a fiercely territorial fish. I have watched spellbound as two large specimens fought like a pair of silent wild dogs for quite some time. These fish can change their color to suit their surroundings or when they feel threatened.

Grunts usually congregate along reefs during the day and feed at night. They are so-named because of the grunting sounds they produce by grinding their molars. Photo: Keith Ibsen.

Grunts

The family of fish known collectively as grunts are so named because of the curious sounds they are able to produce by grinding their molars. Grunts are an important source of food and are not known to harbor any poisonous toxins. They generally feed nocturnally and congregate during the day along the reef. Adults are generally 1-2 feet (31-62 cm) in length.

The **white grunt** (*Haemulon plumieri*) and the **French grunt** (*Haemulon flavolineatum*) are particularly common and often form large shoals. White grunts have a blue and yellow-striped head, and a blue-spotted body. The blue stripes of the French grunt continue along the body from the head.

The **porkfish** (*Anisotremus virginicus*) has a steeper profile than most grunts and has a black stripe running through the eye. Porkfish can grow to lengths of over 1 foot (31 cm) and are often seen in schools. Young porkfish are sometimes found cleaning parasites from other fishes.

Hawksbill Turtle

The **hawksbill turtle** (*Eretmochelys imbricata*) is an endangered species. Artifacts made of tortoiseshell are usually made from the shell of the hawksbill. The name is derived from the hooked-beak appearance of the upper jaw. Found throughout the Caribbean and much sought after for both its shell and its meat, it has been known to contain poisonous toxins. These turtles are very shy and will only approach if they are unaware of a diver's presence. They can weigh up to 100 pounds (46 kg) with the record weight being almost 300 pounds (136 kg).

Moray Eels

The largest of all the Atlantic morays is the **green moray** (*Gymnothorax funebris*) which can grow to lengths of over 6 feet (2 m). Moray eels always look threatening as they must keep their mouths open to breathe and in doing so, bare their sharp teeth. However, there is absolutely nothing to fear from these fish provided they are left alone.

Parrotfishes

Parrotfishes are so named for their parrot-like beaks formed by the fusion of the teeth in their upper and lower jaws. Like wrasses, they swim with pectoral fins, grazing on coral for algae and polyps by day, and resting at night covered in a thick protective mucous. The residue from their crunching, which can be heard by divers, produces fine sand. Parrotfishes go through sex and color changes as they grow; the males usually are quite different from the females. The **stoplight parrotfish** (*Sparisoma viride*) derives its name from the changes in color—from a red belly with brown and white scales in one phase to a predominantly blue-green in another. The **midnight parrotfish** (*Scarus coelestinus*) is dark blue with light blue spots and green teeth. The **blue parrotfish** (*Scarus coeruleus*) is a uniform light to royal blue color with white teeth. The blue is by far the largest of the three, often 3-4 feet (1-1.2 m) long with an occasional supermale over 5 feet (1.5 m) in length. The other varieties range from less than 1 foot (31 cm) to about 30 inches (77 cm). Large parrotfishes are prevalent at Parrotfish Falls and Long Caye Cut.

Porgies

Porgies are generally silvery in color, but may change almost instantly to a mottled pattern. They feed on small shellfish which they are able to grind with their special molars.

The **saucereye porgy** (*Calamus calamus*) is a bright silver color with a steeper profile than others in the same family. It attains a length of up to 15 inches (39 cm). Porgies are good for eating, but they do have many fine bones. They are also a good sport fish.

Rays

The **Atlantic manta** (*Manta birostris*) was undoubtedly the origin of many sea-monster tales among early mariners. With its epic proportions (often over 20 feet [6 m] in wingspan and well over 3,000 pounds [1,364 kg]), and its habit of suddenly breaking the surface, the manta inspired fear that was unearned. In truth, these docile plankton feeders seem barely aware of divers as they cruise some distance off the outer reef, funneling their catch into their mouths with two forward-projecting cephalic fins (hence the nickname "devilfish").

The wing-like pectoral fins of the **spotted eagle ray** (*Aetobatus narinari*) propel them with slow, graceful movements which belie their power. In some of the shallow areas west of the main reef when the sea is calm, these fish can be seen swimming just below the surface. They create a mild wave and their wing tips break the surface together on each upward stroke. Their wingspans can approach 8 feet (2.4 m), and they are often seen swimming in large schools.

Eagle rays, although free-swimming, are bottom feeders, eating mostly mollusks which they crush with their flat jaws. Their caudal spine presents little danger as they do not rest on the bottom where they might be stepped on.

For other rays, see Potentially Harmful Marine Life.

This newly-hatched hawksbill turtle may grow to weigh 100 pounds (45 kg) or more. Because it is an endangered species, it is illegal to bring anything made from its shell into the United States. Photo: Ned Middleton.

This green moray, the largest of all Atlantic morays, is being rid of parasites by cleaning gobies. Photo: Ned Middleton.

Red-banded Coral Shrimp

The **red-banded coral shrimp** (*Stenopus hispidus*) is one of the "cleaner" shrimps which feed off scraps and parasites associated with larger animals. This fascinating creature looks like a miniature lobster. It lives in little holes and gullies, often found upside down on the ceiling. Its long, white antennae may give away its location. They can grow to 4 inches (10 cm).

When approached, the longspine squirrelfish will remain motionless before darting away at the last possible moment. Photo: Keith Ibsen.

Remoras

The **remora** (*Remora remora*) is a "commensal." This describes any species of fish which accompanies the larger specimens such as sharks or rays. They benefit by feeding on the scraps available when the host fish feeds. The remora attaches itself to the host by means of a suction pad on top of its head. In this way it hitches a ride, but can swim freely when it wishes to do so. Once after a dive we found a remora attached to the underside of our boat. Even after speeding to the next dive site at 20 knots, the remora remained attached to the boat.

Spotted Drums

Also called "croakers" for the sound they produce, drums are found in shallow waters and generally are 9 inches (23 cm) to 1 foot (31 cm) in length. The **spotted drum** (*Equetus punctatus*) seems rarer than it is because of its secretive nature. It often hides in little tunnels and caves which are inaccessible to divers. An

extremely pretty fish much sought after by aquarists, it has an elongated front dorsal fin with a white-spotted rear dorsal fin and tail, and a black- and white-striped body.

Squirrelfishes

The **longspine squirrelfish** (*Holocentrus rufus*) is probably the most common of all the squirrelfishes and soldierfishes in Belize. The fish can grow to over 1 foot (31 cm), but is usually found at about half that size. When approached, squirrelfishes will remain motionless until the last possible moment before swimming into the safety of a hole in the coral. Squirrelfishes are nocturnal, and the reddish fish have large eyes for their size. The longspine has white spots along the top of its prominent spiny dorsal fin.

Surgeonfishes

Named for their "scalpels," sharp spines which fold forward at either side of the tail base, surgeonfishes in Belize include the **ocean surgeon** (*Acanthurus bahiaus*), **doctorfish** (*Acanthurus chirurgus*) and **blue tang** (*Acanthurus coeruleus*).

The juvenile blue tang is a bright yellow color which often makes identification confusing. At the intermediate stage the fish is blue with a yellow tail. The adult fish is deep blue all over. Sometimes a yellow fish may be larger than a blue one, as the rate of color change can vary.

Wrasses

This rather extended family of fish is closely related to parrotfishes. Apart from the **hogfish** (*Lachnolaimus maximus*), they are not good for eating. They can often be recognized by their buckteeth and the peculiar "rowing" motion of their pectoral fins.

The hogfish adult male can reach up to 3 feet (1 m) in length and gets its name from its snout. The hogfish is able to change color to suit its background, but the shape of the dorsal fin with its three long dorsal spines will assist with identification.

Potentially Harmful Marine Life

Divers have little to fear from the marine life of Belize, but certain creatures should be approached with some added respect and awareness. There are, however, only a few that are potentially harmful. In almost all instances of injury, the animal was merely acting defensively.

Bristle Worms

The **bristle worm** (*Hermodice carunculata*), also called the fire worm, is not very common in Belize. Any contact with the human body will result in the white bristles embedding themselves under the skin, causing immediate pain. The bristles will also stick to your dive gear and still present a threat after your dive.

Wounds from an injury produce the most excruciating pain and may cause infection. Do not rub the affected area, but apply vinegar liberally and see a doctor if the pain does not subside in a few hours.

Contact with this encrusting stinging coral, the most common of the fire corals, should be avoided. Photo: Ned Middleton.

Fire Corals and Fire Sponges

Fire corals and fire sponges can cause itching, swelling and pain if touched. To avoid persistent discomfort, the diver must learn to recognize these species and practice good buoyancy control to avoid touching them.

Red fire sponge (*Tedania ignis*) looks just as its name describes. It is a flame-red sponge covered with imperceptibly fine hair-like tentacles. It is not very common in Belize, but it can cause the worst symptoms from this group, producing painful swelling and itching.

Other fire corals are a pale yellow-green, and thus are not often recognized by divers until too late.

Encrusting stinging coral (*Millepora alcicornis*) forms dull yellow branches. **Square stinging coral** (*Millepora squarrosa*) has a box-like construction which makes it easily identifiable. **Leafy stinging coral** (*Millepora complanata*) has a fan-like appearance and is less common in Belize.

Fire coral stings are usually painful for only an hour or so, but they can cause a lingering dermatitis in sensitive individuals. Antihistamines, cortisone creams, vinegar and sometimes meat tenderizer can be helpful.

Jellyfishes

The **Portuguese man-of-war** (*Physalia physalis*) derives its name from a contrived similarity with the galleons of the past. It is not a true jellyfish, being more closely related to fire corals and stinging hydroids. The float (or sail) is a shimmering bright blue-purple color which can be up to 8 inches (21 cm) long. The stinging cells contained in the trailing tentacles which may stretch for over 40 feet (12 m) are capable of inflicting extreme pain and even respiratory paralysis.

Divers should stay well clear. If stung, apply vinegar to the area to inactivate the remaining nematocysts. The tentacle should be removed from the skin, taking care not to be stung again. If you help someone else who has been stung, put gloves on first. Do not rub the tentacles with sand as this will only worsen the sting. Antihistamines and cortisone creams may help, but see a doctor immediately.

The **moon jellyfish** (*Aurelia aurita*) is a transparent disk which can grow to over 1 foot (31 cm) across. The disk is fringed with a fine skirt of stinging cells, and although these can cause discomfort there are no lasting ill effects.

Stinging jellyfish (*Dactylometra quinquecirrha*) are a more milky white color with longer stinging tentacles. The disk is usually less than 8 inches (21 cm) across.

Long-Spined Sea Urchin

Any contact with the **long-spined sea urchin** (*Diadema antillarum*) usually results in several pieces of spine becoming embedded under the skin. Unfortunately, once the spines have broken off, they lose their brittleness, making them harder to extract, and they may turn septic. Experienced divers have no trouble avoiding them, but beginners often drop onto them feet first. Make sure your tetanus shot is current and see a doctor if pain persists. Sea urchins are not particularly common in Belize but are likely to be encountered.

Rays

The **southern stingray** (*Dasyatis americana*), **yellow stingray** (*Urolophus jamaicensis*) and the **lesser electric ray** (*Narcine brasiliensis*) all have a serrated spine on the upper surface of the tail. This can be poisonous, but at the very least a stab will cause extreme pain. Stingrays surprise their prey by digging themselves into the sand with just their eyes protruding. It is likely that they will swim off as a diver approaches. However, a wader could accidentally tread on one in shallow water.

The lesser electric ray is able to produce an electric shock for self-defense and to stun prey. The shock is not usually dangerous to divers, but is definitely unpleasant. If left unmolested, rays pose no threat whatsoever to the diver.

Sharks

I have personally seen the following sharks off the coast of Belize: the **American sawshark** (*Pristiophorus schroederi*), **blacktip** (*Carcharhinus limbatus*), **bull** (*Carcharhinus leucas*), **Caribbean reef** (*Carcharhinus peregi*), **great hammerhead** (*Sphyrna mokarran*), **lemon** (*Negaprion brevirostris*), **nurse** (*Ginglymostoma cirratum*) and the **oceanic whitetip** (*Carcharhinus longimanus*). I have also seen the **whale shark** (*Rhiniodon typus*), which, as a plankton feeder, does not feature in any list of dangerous sea creatures. There are few things more exciting to photograph than a shark.

With a modicum of caution and common sense, divers have little to fear from any of these sharks. Spearfishing and molesting resting nurse sharks is inviting trouble, and feeding sharks is best left to those who do it for a living.

Seeing a shark, such as this bull shark, can be an exciting and safe experience, but divers should always be cautious in the presence of sharks. Photo: Ned Middleton.

Stingrays, such as this yellow stingray, have a spine on their tail that can inflict pain if stepped on or touched. Photo: Ned Middleton.

Buoyancy control is especially important to avoid being pierced by a long-spined sea urchin. Their spines easily penetrate skin and can be difficult to remove. Photo: Ned Middleton.

Spotted Scorpionfish

Like other scorpionfishes, the **spotted scorpionfish** (*Scorpaena plumieri*) lacks an air bladder, and thus, buoyancy control. These fish can reach lengths of up to 18 inches (46 cm), but are common at much smaller sizes.

They are found well camouflaged on the bottom, remaining motionless and unseen, and seldom moving except when forced to. When a diver approaches too closely, the fish usually swims off. However, if accidentally touched, it will raise its dorsal fin a moment before contact as its means of defense. Each bony spine within the dorsal fin acts like a hypodermic needle and will pump poison into whatever it penetrates. Wounds from such an injury cause excruciating pain and infection. Soaking the affected area in hot water will help. If the pain persists or one is prone to allergic reactions, consult a doctor.

The well-camouflaged scorpionfish protects itself with venomous spines that can inflict serious damage on divers who inadvertantly step on it or cause it alarm. Photo: Keith Ibsen.

APPENDIX 1

EMERGENCY NUMBERS

Recompression Chamber	**026-2425**
	VHF Marine 68
	VHF 2M 4600

Sub-Aquatic Safety Services, which operates a chamber on Cozumel, opened a two-man, twin-lock recompression chamber in Belize in 1989. It is located at the San Pedro Airport on Ambergris Caye.

To support the chamber leading dive operations charge divers an optional US$1 for each air fill. This fee also provides divers with chamber insurance in the event of an emergency. I recommend you pay this fee to support the chamber even if you have additional insurance.

Police	**911**

Ambulance, Fire	**90**

Hospitals

Belize City
Belize City Hospital	02-31548
Medical Associates	02-30303

Belmopan
Public Hospital	08-22263

Corazol
Corazol Hospital	04-22076

Dangriga
Doctor's Headquarters	05-22084

Orange Walk
Orange Walk Hospital	03-22072

Punta Gorda
Punta Gorda Hospital	07-22026

San Ignacio
San Ignacio Hospital	092-2066

DIVERS ALERT NETWORK (DAN)

The Divers Alert Network (DAN), a non-profit membership organization affiliated with Duke University Medical Center, operates a 24-hour emergency number **(919) 684-8111** (emergencies only) to provide divers and physicians with medical advice on treating diving injuries. DAN can also organize air evacuation to a recompression chamber.

Since many emergency room physicians do not know how to properly treat diving injuries, it is highly recommended that in the event of an accident, you have the physician consult a DAN doctor specializing in diving medicine.

All DAN members receive $100,000 emergency medical evacuation assistance and a subscription to the dive safety magazine, *Alert Diver*. New members receive the DAN *Dive and Travel Medical Guide* and can buy up to $125,000 of dive accident insurance.

DAN offers emergency oxygen first-aid training, and provides funding and consulting for recompression chambers worldwide. They also conduct diving research at Duke University's F.G. Hall Hyperbaric Center.

DAN's address is 3100 Tower Blvd., Suite 1300, Durham, NC 27707. Their non-emergency medical information number is (919) 684-2948. To join call (800) 446-2671.

APPENDIX 2

USEFUL NUMBERS FOR VISITORS

Phone Service

To call Belize from the United States or Canada dial 011-501 plus the local number, leaving out the first zero of the local number.

Information Services

Belize City

Belize Tourist Board	02-77213/73255
83 North Front St.	Fax: 02-77490

United States

Belize Tourist Board	(212) 563-6011
421 Seventh Ave. #1110	(800) 624-0686
New York, NY 10001	Fax: (212) 563-6033

Belize Embassy	(202) 332-9636
2535 Mass. Ave. NW	Fax: (202) 332-6888
Washington, D.C. 20008	

Belize Mission To The U.N.	(212) 599-0233
820 Second Ave., # 922	Fax: (212) 599-3391
New York, NY 10017	

Domestic Airlines

Island Air	02-31140/02-31707
Javier's Flying Service	02-45332
Maya Airways	02-44234/026-2611
Tropic Air	02-45671/026-2012

Car Rentals
(in Belize City unless otherwise noted)

Alistair King, Punta Gorda	07-22126
Avis Rent-A-Car	025-2629
Budget Rent-A-Car	02-32435
Country Tours	02-33292
Crystal Auto Rental	02-31600
Elijah Sutherland	02-73582
Gordon Lionel	02-72184
Jabiru Auto Rental	02-44680
Jaguar	02-73142/025-2747
National Car Rental	02-31650/02-32637
Pancho's	025-2540/02-45554
Safari	02-35395/02-30886
Smith & Sons	02-73779
Tour Belize	02-71271
Tropical Adventure	025-2708

Other Numbers of Interest

Audubon Society Belize City	02-34987
British High Commision 34/36 Halfmoon Ave. Belmopan	08-22146
Center for Environmental Studies Belize City	02-45739
Department of Archaelology Belmopan	08-22106
Marine Terminal (ferry service)	02-31969
Rain Forest Research Institute Maskall Village	03-22199
U.S. Embassy, Consular Section 29 Gabourel Lane Belize City	02-77161
Weather Bureau	025-2012

APPENDIX 3

DIVE OPERATIONS

Belize City

Aggressor Fleet, Ltd.
Tel: (800) 348-2868

Belize Dive Connection
Tel: 02-34526

Blackline Dive Shop
Tel: 02-44155

Blue Planet Divers
Tel: 02-76770

Caribbean Charter Services
Tel: 02-30404

**Maya Landings Marina
/Dive Belize**
Tel: 02-45798
Fax: 02-30263

Peter Hughes Diving, Inc.
Tel: (800) 932-6237

**Ramada Royal Reef Resort
& Marina**
Tel: (800) 854-7854

**Radisson Fort George
Marina**
Tel: 02-33333

Caye Caulker

Belize Diving Service, Ltd.
Tel: 022-2143

Frenchie's Diving Services
Tel: 022-2234

Ambergris Caye

Amigos Del Mar
Tel: 026-2648

Belize Dive Center
Tel: 026-2797

Coral Beach Dive Shop
Tel: 026-2013

Danny's Divers
Tel: 026-2437

Hustler Tours
Tel: 026-2538

Paradise Dive Club
Tel: 026-2739

Ramon's Dive Shop
Tel: 026-2071

Reef Divers I
Tel: 026-2965

Reef Divers II
Tel: 026-3133

Rubie's Hotel Dive Shop
Tel: 026-2063

**San Pedro Dive &
Snorkel Center**
Tel: 026-2982

The Dive Shop, Ltd.
Tel: 026-2437

Tortuga Dive Center
Tel: 026-2018

Victoria House Dive Shop
Tel: 026-2067

Placencia

Kingfisher Sports, Ltd
Tel: 06-23104

Rum Point Inn
Tel: 06-23239

Offshore Atoll Island Operations

Blue Marlin Lodge
Tel: 05-22243

Glovers Atoll Resort
Tel: 05-23048

Indigo Divers
Tel: (800) 468-0123

Lighthouse Reef Resort
Tel: 02-31205

Manta Resort
Tel: 02-31895

Spanish Bay Resort
Tel: 02-72725

St. George's Lodge
Tel: 02-44190

Turneffe Flats
Tel: 02-30116

Turneffe Island Lodge
Tel: 02-30116

INDEX

A **bold** faced page number denotes a picture caption.
An <u>underlined</u> page number indicates detailed treatment.

FREE CATALOG

Aqua Quest Publications, Inc. publishes and distributes a full line of books on underwater photography, wreck diving, marine life, travel destinations, technical diving and safety. If these books are not available at your local book or dive store please write or call us directly for a catalog of our publications.

AQUA QUEST PUBLICATIONS, INC.
Post Office Box A
Locust Valley, NY 11560-0495

1-800-933-8989   **516-759-0476**